PHILANTHROPARTIES!

PHILANTHROPARTIES!

A Party-Planning Guide for Kids Who Want to Give Back

LULU CERONE

ALADDIN
New York London Toronto Sydney New Delhi

BEYOND WORDS
Hillsboro, Oregon

ALADDIN
An imprint of Simon & Schuster
Children's Publishing Division
1230 Avenue of the Americas
New York, NY 10020

BEYOND WORDS
20827 N.W. Cornell Road, Suite 500
Hillsboro, Oregon 97124-9808
503-531-8700 / 503-531-8773 fax
www.beyondword.com

This Beyond Words/Aladdin hardcover edition May 2017
Text and photography copyright © 2017 by Sofia Lulu Cerone
Cover design copyright © 2017 by Beyond Words/Simon & Schuster, Inc.
Cover photos copyright © 2017 by Sofia Lulu Cerone

ALADDIN and related logo are registered trademarks of Simon & Schuster, Inc.
BEYOND WORDS PUBLISHING and related logo are registered trademarks of Beyond Words
Publishing. Beyond Words is an imprint of Simon & Schuster, Inc.

For information about special discounts for bulk purchases, please contact Simon & Schuster
Special Sales at 1-866-506-1949 or business@simonandschuster.com.

The Simon & Schuster Speakers Bureau can bring authors to your live event. For more information or to
book an event contact the Simon & Schuster Speakers Bureau at 1-866-248-3049 or visit our website at
www.simonspeakers.com.

Managing Editor: Lindsay S. Easterbrooks-Brown
Copyeditor: Linda M. Meyer
Proofreader: Kristin Thiel
Contributing writer: Lucy Keating
Photography: Renee Bowen
Interior and cover design: Sara E. Blum
The text of this book was set in Adobe Garamond Pro, Lunchbox, and Avenir LT Std.

Manufactured in China 0717 SCP

10 9 8 7 6 5 4 3 2

Library of Congress Cataloging-in-Publication Data

Names: Cerone, Lulu, author.
Title: Philanthroparties! : a party-planning guide for kids who want to give
  back / Lulu Cerone.
Description: New York : Aladdin ; Hillsboro, Oregon : Beyond Words, 2017. |
Includes bibliographical references.
Identifiers: LCCN 2016037987 | ISBN 9781582705873 (hardcover)
Subjects: LCSH: Young volunteers in social service—Juvenile literature. |
  Young volunteers in community development—Juvenile literature. | Special
  events—Planning—Juvenile literature. | Charities—Juvenile literature.
Classification: LCC HV40.42 .C47 2017 | DDC 361.7—dc23
LC record available at https://lccn.loc.gov/2016037987

Dedicated to Dr. Jeni Stepanek, who has taught me to live
each day with purpose and always remember to play.

CONTENTS

A PERCENTAGE OF THE PROCEEDS FROM THE SALE OF THIS BOOK WILL PROVIDE SCHOLARSHIPS FOR GIRLS IN DEVELOPING COUNTRIES THROUGH LEMONAID WARRIOR'S EDUCATION PROJECTS.

BECOMING A YOUNG PHILANTHROPIST

Hello, social activist! Thank you for picking up my book. I'm so happy you did. If you're reading this, it's because, like me, you want to help people. And this book is going to show you how to do it. Inside you will find over thirty different ways to make philanthropy—the practice of helping others—a part of your everyday life, through parties, recipes, games, and activities. I hope they inspire some awesome ideas! But first, I want to tell you a story.

In the late afternoon on January 12, 2010, a 7.0 earthquake hit the Caribbean island nation of Haiti, just outside its capital of Port-au-Prince. Everyone knows that earthquakes can be really damaging, and 7.0 on the Richter scale is categorized as "major." Many thousands of people in Haiti lost their homes, their access to food and water, their loved ones—everything.

This horrible tragedy triggered a strong emotional response in me. I remember seeing images online and on television that brought me to tears. People, including kids my age, were living among rubble that had once been their homes. I'd never been exposed to such a global tragedy before, and I knew I had to help.

There was just one problem: I was only ten years old. This earthquake was a massive humanitarian issue, affecting two million people, and it was thousands of miles from my home. I felt powerless. I didn't think I could make a difference.

But I didn't let that stop me.

I grew up in a suburb of Los Angeles, California, in a tight-knit family, with parents who have always encouraged my younger brother Jasper and me to give back. Living where we do, it can get pretty hot in the summer (over a hundred degrees Fahrenheit!), so I'd had my fair share of lemonade stands over the years. In fact, I was pretty much a pro. Instead of saying we could buy ice cream or toys with our earnings, my parents always encouraged my brother and me to use the money to help other people or to fix problems in our community. Lemonade stands were my introduction to philanthropy and to the rewarding feeling that comes with doing good.

So there I was, desperate to find a way to make a difference in Haiti, to help in any way I could. Naturally, I turned to lemonade stands. But this problem was huge, and I knew I needed to get others involved. I decided to add a bit of competition to make things more exciting. I organized a LemonAID War: a girls-versus-boys lemonade stand contest to see who could raise the most money in two weeks. One email to my fifth-grade class was all it took, and we were in business. Everyone wanted to join.

And guess what? We raised $4,000 for the earthquake victims! I was stunned. It felt great. What's more, it was the social highlight of the year. Because we weren't just giving back—we were having fun. We realized, as ten-year-olds, that we already had the power to create change and even save lives, and we didn't want to stop! If a lemonade stand could help people in need and inspire my entire class to keep doing more, then I knew I was onto something.

The LemonAID War opened our eyes to the needs around us, and after it, whenever my friends heard about a disaster or somebody in need, they would ask me to plan another event like the LemonAID War. I also had a new curiosity to find out more about world issues. I became particularly interested in the global water crisis. While I could easily turn on a tap and enjoy a refreshing glass of water anytime I wanted, I learned that girls like me across the globe had to walk for hours in the hot sun and along dangerous paths to retrieve dirty water for their families. I was shocked that so many people were living without such a basic necessity, and, again, I knew I had to help. As I learned from my LemonAID War, I needed to come up with a way to unite my friends, raise money, and, of course, have fun. Then I had an idea that changed everything. My birthday was around the corner. I thought, why don't I throw a water-themed birthday party, and instead of presents, ask for donations to help a charity build a water well?

In that moment, I realized that I had just come up with the perfect formula to combine doing good with having a good time: PhilanthroParties. With a simple twist, I transformed my regular old birthday party into a chance to raise money and awareness for a cause that I was passionate about. The party was such a success that we ended up raising enough money to build a well in Africa, and the party became an annual event! You can read more about this party under the July section on page 90.

But why stop at birthday parties? Any party or social gathering can be effective with a few small tweaks. And just imagine how many different causes PhilanthroParties can support! It has become my goal to help those in my generation find causes that speak to them—like the earthquake in Haiti and the global water crisis spoke to me—and then give them the tools to channel that compassion and make social activism a part of their social lives. Plus, I have found that when you're having a great time doing good, you'll want to do it again and again. It might even become a habit that you continue throughout the rest of your life.

In 2011 I started a nonprofit organization called LemonAID Warriors to share my ideas for PhilanthroParties and encourage other kids to throw their own events. So far, LemonAID Warriors has inspired PhilanthroParties around the world, and my personal parties have raised over $100,000 to support various local and global causes. This book showcases thirty-six of our most successful and unique PhilanthroParties, along with thirty-six recipes, fifty-four games and activities, and thirty-two crafts to get you started. If you aren't already accustomed to using a stove, oven, or sharp kitchen or craft tool, make sure an adult is present. I hope these ideas spark your creativity and compassion and that you see how easy it is to make giving a fun part of your life!

WHAT IS A PHILANTHROPARTY, EXACTLY?

A PhilanthroParty is a party with a purpose. It's what happens when you connect *hanging out* with *helping out*. It means picking a cause you care about, choosing a celebration or gathering, and combining the two for the ultimate social event. To get you started on creating your own unique PhilanthroParty, take a look at my easy three-step guide for turning your passion into action:

1. *Pick a cause.* What speaks to your heart? What do you see in your everyday life and wish you could change? Think closer to home, like in your own community, or think bigger, like somewhere else in the world. No issue is too small or too big, but the cause you choose should really speak to you personally. If you don't know what it is yet, don't worry. And don't be afraid to try a few things until you feel that spark of compassion.

2. *Pick a date.* Take a look at your calendar. If it's like mine, there's rarely any free time, but don't let that stop you! What are you already doing this month or next? A birthday party, a holiday celebration, or even a simple sleepover can be turned into something that has social impact and makes giving part of the fun. Need more inspiration? Take a look at our list of holidays, some of them wacky, at the beginning of every chapter. Be sure to check with anyone you are counting on to be there. You don't want previous commitments to prevent your friends from attending, and the same goes for representatives of a charity or organization, or any other special guests you might want to invite.

3. *Pick an activity.* Now comes the really fun part. One idea is to choose an activity inspired by the cause you've chosen to support. Do you love dogs and you're hosting a sleepover? Make homemade dog treats with your friends to donate to a local shelter. Another source of inspiration, as you'll see in many of our parties, is the holiday itself. Planning on hosting a party on Earth Day? Organize a park cleanup and then have a picnic! It can be that simple.

Now, if you find yourself having trouble making a decision about any of the steps above (or if you aren't finding a party example within this book that speaks to you), no problem. Here are some easy, foolproof PhilanthroParty pairing ideas.

CAUSE	EVENT	ACTIVITY
Water crisis	Birthday	Ask for donations to fund wells instead of birthday presents.
Hospitalized children	Valentine's Day	Make inspirational cards for patients in a children's hospital.
Homelessness	Sleepover	Ask guests to bring gently used blankets to donate to a homeless shelter.
Education	School dance	Talk to your student council about accepting school supplies as admission to the dance for a local drive.
Environment	Beach day	Trash scavenger hunt! Award prizes for the most bottles, plastic, metal, etc.
Hunger	Summer barbecue	Ask guests to bring five cans each for a local food bank.

MORE HELPFUL TIPS ON PICKING A CAUSE

Here are more places to look for inspiration when trying to pick the cause you want to take on for your PhilanthroParty.

1. *Your own life.* Have you or a loved one experienced a major obstacle or a crisis? Can you think of a time when you needed help? Personal stories of illness or tragedy can inspire you to help people who are going through something similar.

2. *Your local community.* In your daily life, do you see something that always bothers you? Maybe you pass the same homeless person on the street or see an elderly neighbor struggle with taking out the trash every week. Reach out and connect with problems that are right in front of you. Start with small things and see where they lead.

3. *Your global community.* Did you read something in the news or see a video or photo about a crisis far away that upset you? It may not be an issue that affects you directly, but maybe it gave you a lump in your throat or made you want to scream. These sensations are your body's way of telling you to take action. It's your compassion calling and leading you to your cause.

4. *Your school.* Don't forget about your school as a place for social activism inspiration. I've found that history, social studies, and science classes are filled with stories of injustice that might motivate you to take action as part of your classwork or as a school project. Some fifth-grade English students wrote me once to say that they were moved by a passage describing an elephant in misery, in the book *The Giver* by Lois Lowry. So all the students who had a birthday that month decided to have a combined PhilanthroParty, and they started a petition against poaching. They asked that instead of presents they receive donations to support an elephant sanctuary.

5. *Your hobbies.* Your passions and extracurricular activities can inspire action. My soccer team brought their gently used cleats to an end-of-season party and donated them to the US Soccer Foundation, which distributes soccer equipment to people in underserved communities. Or maybe knitting is your thing. Invite your knitting club over for tea and cookies, and then teach them to knit tiny thumb socks that make it impossible for drivers to text and drive. It's fun and silly, but it just might save a life.

So there you go! That's my story. The main thing I've learned from what I've done so far? Trust your ideas—no matter how small or how crazy they may seem—and don't feel confined by your age. You already have the capacity to make change. What are you waiting for? Let's PhilanthroParty!

Lulu Cerone

JANUARY

HERE ARE SOME MORE NATIONAL CELEBRATORY
THEMES FOR THE MONTH OF JANUARY.

Braille Literacy Month
Blood Donor Month
New Year's Day—January 1
Dress Up Your Pet Day—January 14
Pie Day—January 23
Handwriting Day—January 23
Opposite Day—January 25
Chocolate Cake Day—January 27
Puzzle Day—January 29
Backward Day—January 31
Chinese New Year—date varies, January or February

1

Martin Luther King Jr. Day: "I Have a Dream" After-Service Party

CELEBRATE YOUR DAY OF SERVICE.

Change starts with a dream, and Dr. Martin Luther King Jr.'s dream was to live in a society where everyone would be treated equally, regardless of skin color. His famous "I Have a Dream" speech guided the civil rights movement in the 1960s, a movement that pushed to end racial discrimination. Dr. King's dream transformed America. What's your dream?

As I mentioned earlier, in January 2010 my dream was to help the victims of an earthquake that caused massive destruction throughout Haiti. The earthquake happened to occur the

week before Martin Luther King Jr. Day—the third Monday in January—when thousands of Americans celebrate his birthday by fulfilling their dreams of a better world through service. I spent that MLK Day weekend throwing my girls-versus-boys LemonAID War, which was my first-ever fundraiser. This event sparked my passion for social activism and led me to start my own organization. And it all started with a dream.

This MLK Day, it's your turn to dream. What issues do you connect with? What do you want to fix in your community? Your country? The world? The cool thing about dreams is that there's no limit to them. Maybe your dream is to end world hunger or put a stop to gender inequality. Maybe it's to make the world less lonely for someone or bring comfort to animals without a home. Whatever it may be, MLK Day is the perfect opportunity to create change and, of course, to party!

Encourage your friends, classmates, and others in your community to follow in Dr. King's footsteps and turn their dreams into action. Host an "I Have a Dream" After-Service Party for those who spent the day doing something good, whether it be volunteering, fundraising, or completing another activity to better their communities or the world. Create a Twitter and Instagram hashtag for people to use when posting photos of their progress throughout the day. Admission to the party is proof of service!

HASHTAG IDEAS

#MyMLKDay
#DayONnotDayOFF
#MLKDayON
#DOtheDream
#MyMountainTop
#MLKDayDreams

DOING THE DREAM

So where do you begin once you decide to throw an "I Have a Dream" After-Service Party? Here are ideas to get you dreaming and doing. Remember, these are just suggestions. Let your creativity guide you.

"I HAVE A DREAM" BULLETIN BOARD[1]

Here's a creative way to help everyone connect with Dr. King's message at the end of the day by allowing them to reflect on and express their dreams for a better future.

What You Need

- Foam board
- Fabric (8 inches longer and wider than the board)
- Tape measure
- Packing tape
- A length of ribbon or cord (optional)
- Pushpins
- Notecards or blank stickers
- Pens or markers
- Small frames or other decorative items (optional)

How to Make It

1. Start with a foam board and fabric of your choice. You can buy a foam board at most craft or office supply stores, or you can reuse a trifold foam board that was once used for a school project. If you don't already have fabric in your house, stop by a local fabric store for an inexpensive remnant. You shouldn't need much more than a yard.

2. Measure your board and then measure your fabric, making sure that the fabric is 8 inches longer and wider than the board. Cut your fabric accordingly. If there are folds or wrinkles in the fabric, ironing is recommended.

3. Lay the fabric facedown and flat on the floor or a table. Place the foam board facedown on top of the fabric. Center the board by using a ruler to measure 4 inches of fabric on all sides.

4. On the bottom, fold the excess fabric toward the center. Tape the length of the fabric edge to the board.

5. Choose a corner. Neatly fold the excess fabric as you would wrap the corner of a gift with wrapping paper.

6. Fold the excess fabric along the side toward the center and tape the length of the fabric edge to the board.

7. Repeat for all corners and sides. It's very important that the fabric is taut, so make sure you pull it tightly before you tape it down.

> "I HAVE A DREAM THAT . . . EVERYONE WILL HAVE A ROOF TO SLEEP BENEATH."

8. Optional: If you want to hang your board for display, use a staple gun to secure a looped piece of ribbon or cord to the back; it should be slightly longer than the length of your board.

9. For the final touch, I used stickers to spell the word *Dream*, but you could also make a sign that says, *I have a dream that . . .* and pin it to the top of the board. Voila! You have your super-cute "I Have a Dream" board.

10. During your After-Service Party, set out notecards, pens or markers, optional decorative items, and pushpins, so people can write down their dreams and pin them to the board.

FOOD FOR THOUGHT

It's known that Dr. King was a man who loved pecan pie and Southern comfort food. To go with this yummy, gooey pic, you can serve cold fried chicken, sweet potato fries, or other Southern favorites. It's like a picnic in January!

MLK JR.'S FAVORITE PECAN PIE
{Makes 1 pie; serves 8 slices}

PIECRUST

What You Need

- 2½ sticks (1¼ cups) cold unsalted butter
- 2½ cups all-purpose flour
- 1 teaspoon salt
- 2 teaspoons granulated sugar
- ½ cup sour cream (regular, not low-fat)

How to Make It

1. Cut the butter into roughly ¼-inch cubes. Place it in the freezer to keep it as cold as possible while you measure the dry ingredients.

2. In a large bowl, whisk together the flour, salt, and sugar.

3. Scatter the chilled cubes of butter over the flour mixture. Use your hands to squish the dry ingredients and butter together until the mixture resembles a coarse meal (leave a few tiny chunks of butter).

4. Using a fork, stir the sour cream into the mixture. Avoid overworking the dough; it's totally fine to leave some streaks of sour cream in it.

5. Gather the dough into a ball. Cut the ball in half and form each half into a flat circle, about 5 inches across.

"I HAVE A DREAM THAT . . . EVERY GIRL WILL HAVE A CHANCE TO GO TO SCHOOL."

"I HAVE A DREAM THAT . . . NOBODY WILL GO HUNGRY ANYMORE."

What's your dream?

6. Lightly sprinkle each dough circle all over with flour. Wrap tightly with plastic wrap and chill in the refrigerator for at least 30 minutes. (You can do this up to a day ahead of making the actual pie.)

7. After it's done chilling, you are ready to roll out the dough. Sprinkle a clean, flat surface with a little flour to prevent sticking. Use a rolling pin to roll the dough into a 9- to 10-inch circle. Loosely fold the dough and sprinkle with flour before kneading it back into a ball. At this point, the streaks of sour cream should be worked in, so the dough has a nice, uniform texture. Now roll it out to an even thickness, 12 to 14 inches wide.

8. Place the rolled crust onto a pie plate. Press it evenly into the bottom and up the sides, leaving a ½ inch overhang. Fold the overhang under at the rim of the pie plate. Crimp or flute the edge of the crust to your liking.

9. Put the crust in the freezer for 30 minutes while you make the yummy pie filling.

PECAN PIE FILLING

What You Need

1½ cups chopped pecans
3 large eggs
1 cup granulated sugar
¾ cup light or dark corn syrup
2 tablespoons butter, melted
2 teaspoons vanilla extract
½ teaspoon salt

How to Make It

1. Preheat oven to 350°F.

2. On a baking sheet, spread pecans in a single layer and bake for 8 to 10 minutes or until lightly toasted.

3. In a large bowl, stir together eggs, sugar, corn syrup, melted butter, vanilla extract, and salt. Stir in pecans.

4. Pour filling into frozen pie shell.

5. Bake for 55 minutes or until set, shielding top of pie with aluminum foil after 20 minutes to prevent excessive browning. Serve warm.

2
National Soup Month: Soup-er Hero PhilanthroParty

MAKE SOUP TO WARM THE HEARTS OF THE HUNGRY.

I believe that soup has powers. Or should I say, *soup*-er powers? Just one bowl can provide immediate comfort, whether you need to warm up on a chilly day or you're soothing an upset tummy. (Chicken soup is actually medicinal and can help heal colds!) Soup reminds me of winter days at my grandparents' house in Canada. After my brother, Jasper, and I played in the snow for hours with our cousins, our grandma would always have a steaming pot of homemade soup waiting for us inside.

Jasper cares deeply about helping the homeless, so I introduced him to my friend Katie Stagliano. Katie's organization, called Katie's Krops, gives kids grants to start gardens and use the food that they grow to feed the homeless in their communities. Jasper decided to start a Katie's Krops garden of his own. After doing some research, he also found a local shelter that doesn't have anyone to cook for them on the weekends due to lack of funding. Their guidelines allowed for donations of home-cooked foods, so Jasper had the idea to get his friends together for a cooking PhilanthroParty. Using the tomatoes from his garden, they had a great time making tomato gazpacho and delivering it to the shelter.

This January, celebrate National Soup Month by being a *soup*-er hero and feeding those without food. Get some friends together and have a soup-making party! Cooking and delivering soup is the perfect way to strengthen friendships and really see the difference that you're making in your community. Plus, for those who are disasters in the kitchen (like me), soup doesn't require a lot of culinary skill, particularly our no-cook gazpacho recipe below.

SOUP-ER PARTY PREP

Remember to start planning your party by doing research. Call some local homeless shelters and soup kitchens to confirm that they can accept donations of homemade soup. And find out the best days and times to deliver the soup to ensure that it can be eaten within twenty-four hours, just to be safe. Also ask if they need an ingredient list provided in case some of the residents have dietary restrictions.

Once you have the charity and its guidelines squared away, ask each friend to bring an ingredient to add to the soup. Create a document on Google Docs with a column down one side listing ingredients, and email the link to the list of attendees. Have everyone fill in their name next to an item.

> WHAT MATTERS IS THE SOUP ITSELF, BUT I THINK THAT JARS WORK GREAT FOR PRESENTATION. YOU CAN USUALLY FIND MASON JARS AT BULK STORES, DOLLAR STORES, OR HOBBY STORES. IF YOU DON'T FIND ANY, PLASTIC FOOD STORAGE CONTAINERS WORK FINE TOO.

FOOD HANDLING AND TRANSPORTING THE SOUP

Before you start making soup with your friends, be sure that the containers you use to transport the soup to the shelter are sterile and that you handle both the containers and all food prep with clean hands. Wash each container in a dishwasher or wash them in hot, soapy water, rinsing them off and letting them air-dry completely before filling with your yummy soup. You can also wear gloves when handling food, and make sure to keep your hair on your head, not in the food. See the PhilanthroParty Checklist (page 182) for more food-safety tips.

PHRASES FOR YOUR LABELS

Stirred with Love
Seasoned with Care
Cold Comfort
JARS OF JOY
Soup's On!

LABEL WITH LOVE

It's time to have fun creating unique labels with your party guests. Set up a label-making table and write positive messages for the residents at the shelter. Label stickers work great for every type of container. If you're presenting your soup in mason jars, consider using tags for a different look. Check out these decorating ideas for inspiration.

1. *Ribbon or string.* Set out colorful string or ribbon for your guests to tie around the containers for an extra decorative element. This works best for the necks of jars.

2. *Tomato cutout.* If you follow our recipe for Jasper's Easy Garden Gazpacho, here's a *soup*-er idea: Cut tomato shapes out of red and green paper or craft felt. Glue the tomato to your jar (if you use felt, use tacky glue).

3. *Chalkboard labels.* Normal white labels work great, but chalkboard labels are a cool alternative. Write your message with chalk or permanent markers and then stick the chalkboard labels on your jars.

4. *Washi tape.* To liven up your label, use washi tape to make a border. Invented in Japan, washi is like masking tape, but it's made of natural fibers and is available in tons of colors and patterns. You can get it on Etsy and other online marketplaces or in craft stores.

5. *Jar lid labels.* If you use jars for your soup, you might like to decorate the lids rather than the jars. Before your guests arrive, measure the jar lids and cut circular templates out of cardboard or thick paper. Provide scissors and colored or patterned paper, as well as markers and other art supplies (but avoid glitter, as it can get into the food). Trace your templates onto paper and then cut out and decorate your circular labels before gluing them to the lids.

FOOD FOR THOUGHT

Gazpacho is a Spanish-style soup made from a tomato base with other vegetables and spices, served cold. There's absolutely no cooking involved, which makes it an easy soup to make with a larger group, and the shelter doesn't have to heat it before serving. The recipe below only makes around 6 cups of soup, so you're going to need to make a few batches. Find out how many people you're serving and plan accordingly.

JASPER'S EASY GARDEN GAZPACHO
{Makes 6 cups of soup}

What You Need

Plastic food storage containers
   or mason jars (six 8-ounce mason
   jars for every 6 cups of soup)
Blender
2 pounds cherry tomatoes
1 medium cucumber, peeled and roughly
   chopped
½ yellow bell pepper, roughly chopped
2 thick, stale bread slices, torn into pieces
¼ cup olive oil
2 tablespoons red wine vinegar
1 garlic clove
1 tablespoon lemon juice
1 cup water

How to Make It

1. Have your containers and blender ready to go before you prepare your ingredients.

2. Place all ingredients in the blender and blend to desired consistency. More time for smooth, less time for chunky.

3. Fill your containers and refrigerate for up to 24 hours before taking them to the shelter. Make enough batches of soup to serve all residents of the shelter. It's that easy!

National Popcorn Day:
Movie Night for the Troops

LIGHTS, CAMERA, TAKE ACTION: ENJOY A MOVIE NIGHT AND DVD DRIVE TO BENEFIT SOLDIERS.

Some of my favorite childhood memories involve a movie, a group of friends or family, and an old projector. I still remember when my dad brought the projector home. My brother and I stared at the heavy silver box as if it were an ancient artifact. It soon became a beloved object, and we spent weekends hosting backyard screenings for our friends. We'd cozy up with blankets and hot cocoa in the winter and enjoy movies by the pool in the summer. Now it's one of our favorite family traditions.

Watching movies is a national pastime in America. However, the men and women in the military fighting for our country don't get to enjoy movies like we at home do. Fortunately, organizations like DVDs4Vets and AMVETS send DVDs overseas to our troops. The act goes beyond entertainment value. Often, watching a movie is the only diversion soldiers get for weeks at a

LULU'S FAVORITE MOVIES

The Iron Giant

Shrek

The Lion King

Grease

The Virgin Suicides

Moonrise Kingdom

Dazed and Confused

Ferris Bueller's Day Off

Juno

Kill Bill

Ghost World

Fast Times at Ridgemont High

Remember, not all these movies are for all ages, so be sure to ask a parent or guardian if you're not sure.

time. With so many movies available on demand these days, we all have DVDs lying around that we probably won't use again. How about donating them to soldiers who will?

Everybody knows that a trip to the movies is so not worth it unless a huge bag of buttery popcorn is involved. So celebrate National Popcorn Day on January 19 by hosting your very own movie night, complete with friends and lots of popcorn. The price of admission: DVD donations for soldiers!

OPERATION MOVIE NIGHT

Your first step is to decide how you'll show the movie. If you have access to a movie projector, that's awesome! You can even look into renting one if your parents agree. Then you'll need a flat surface to project the movie onto. You can rent a screen, use a blank wall, or even just hang a white sheet on a fence or the side of your house. I repurposed my lemonade stand to use as a film screen. (You'll notice that I find many uses for my lemonade stand in my PhilanthroParties.)

Backyard movies are fun, but if January is a cold month where you live, an inside showing works too. If you don't have access to a projector, use your television. In either case, make sure to clear out your living room to make space for your guests. It can be fun to put a mattress on the floor and pile it high with pillows and blankets for cozy viewing. Invite your guests to come in pajamas or other comfortable clothes.

SETTING THE SCENE

Once you have prepped all the treats and craft items (don't worry; I'll tell you how to do that in a minute), set the party scene. Place the fresh popcorn, paper bags, and fancy fixin's on a table next to your art supplies and a box for the DVD donations. When your guests arrive, invite them to decorate their popcorn bags and donate their movies (with or without notes to those serving in the military). When it's movie time, everyone can fill their bag with popcorn and pick their fixin's to sprinkle on top. Lights, camera, action!

DECORATE PAPER BAGS

For a little pre-movie fun, make festive popcorn bags. Set out brown paper lunch bags, markers, and stickers and then encourage guests to personalize their popcorn bags.

What You Need

Brown paper lunch bags
Markers
Sticker labels

Individual popcorn bags are more hygienic than grabbing from a communal bowl.

If you feel inspired, use the markers and stickers to also write notes of thanks or encouragement that you can slip into the donated movies.

PERSONALIZED POPCORN

Popcorn is a quintessential treat for any movie night and it can be easily fancied up and personalized with a fixin's station. Make enough plain, lightly salted popcorn for your party guests. Then, set up a popcorn bar with the fresh popcorn and a buffet of interesting fixin's. Write out and display instructions that give your guests suggestions about customizing their popcorn.

FANCY POPCORN FIXIN'S: MOVIE CANDY POPCORN MIX-INS

What You Need

Movie candy
Honey roasted nuts (optional)

What to Do

Sweet-and-salty can be a delicious combination. Set out individual bowls of movie candy such as M&M's, Raisinets, licorice, and, my favorite, honey roasted peanuts. Invite guests to toss them with the popcorn in their personalized popcorn bag.

FANCY POPCORN FIXIN'S: CINNAMON & SUGAR POPCORN

What You Need

1 cup granulated sugar
4 tablespoons ground cinnamon
Butter spray

What to Do

Mix sugar and cinnamon together and place it in an empty spice shaker for people to toss on popcorn. (Spooning it out of a bowl works just fine if you don't have a shaker.) Instruct guests to squirt some butter spray on the popcorn in their bags, sprinkle the cinnamon sugar on top, fold the bag tops closed, and then shake their bags.

FANCY POPCORN FIXIN'S: ROSEMARY PARMESAN POPCORN

What You Need

Fresh rosemary sprigs (you'll need around 3–4 sprigs per guest)
1 cup finely grated parmesan cheese
Butter spray

How to Make It

1. Preheat the oven to 300°F.

2. On a baking sheet, bake fresh rosemary sprigs for 10 minutes. Let them cool.

3. Strip the narrow leaves off the stems, discard the stems, and finely chop the crispy leaves.

4. In a bowl, toss the rosemary with the parmesan.

5. Instruct guests to squirt some butter spray on the popcorn in their bags, sprinkle with the rosemary parmesan, fold the bag tops closed, and then shake it, shake it, shake it!

FEBRUARY

ADDITIONAL FEBRUARY EVENTS

HERE ARE SOME MORE NATIONAL CELEBRATORY
THEMES FOR THE MONTH OF FEBRUARY.

American Heart Month

Black History Month

Children's Dental Health Month

National Wear Red Day—first Friday in February

Groundhog Day—February 2

Thank a Mailman Day—February 4

Send a Card to a Friend Day—February 7

Boy Scouts Day (Scout Sunday)—the Sunday before February 8

White T-Shirt Day—February 11

Make a Friend Day—February 11

Lincoln's Birthday—February 12

Love Your Pet Day—February 20

National Tortilla Chip Day—February 24

Carnival Day—February 26

Tell a Fairy Tale Day—February 26

Mardi Gras—date varies, February or March

Oscar Night—date varies, February or March

4

Valentine's Day:
Spread the Love PhilanthroParty

SPREAD LOVE AT A WOMEN'S SHELTER WITH PAMPERING FOR THE MOMS AND CRAFTS FOR THE KIDS.

Ahh, Valentine's Day, an international celebration of love. To some, Valentine's Day means a box of chocolates or hoping for a card from someone special. To others, it means ice cream and laughs with good friends and a romantic comedy. Whether or not it involves an actual valentine, February 14 is the perfect day to share your love with family, friends, and others who might need a little extra.

One Valentine's Day, my warriors and I threw a party at a local shelter that houses women and children who are victims of domestic violence. Valentine's Day is particularly tough for the women at the shelter, so we entertained the kids and gave the women a break from their mom duties by treating them to a night of relaxation. We brought food, decorated the patio, and set up a cookie-decorating table and card-making station, where we made cards for kids at a nearby children's hospital. Helping other people is an empowering, confidence-building experience for everyone, and the kids at the shelter were no exception. They loved making the cards and feeling the joy of helping other kids who were going through a tough time. It also broke the ice between the volunteers and the kids at the shelter. Instead of feeling like we were helping them, they also felt like they were helping us with our card project. Making cards together put us on equal ground and gave us a common goal.

As part of our Valentine's Day Party, we asked a massage therapist to donate her time to help pamper the moms. We didn't realize that some of the women wouldn't be comfortable being touched. One woman in particular was very nervous to get a massage, but all of her friends from the shelter stood by her side, and slowly she allowed the therapist to massage her hand, then her arm, and then her shoulders. Fortunately, this was a positive experience and a big breakthrough moment for her, but it taught us to think through our ideas in the future. What might seem like a good idea in the moment could create challenges for the people we are hoping to help. Doing your research and asking in-depth questions is very important in the planning process.

To add yet another element of pampering for the moms, we invited the Polished Girlz to give manicures.

Polished Girlz is an organization that was founded by Alanna Wall when she was ten years old. She supplies nail polish kits to teams of manicurists who donate services to people in need. Fortunately for us, Alanna had a team of volunteers in Los Angeles, and they were able to come help us out. Anyone can invite the Polished Girlz to lend a hand at an event or outreach program. And if you want to *be* a Polished Girl, you can email her about that too. By the way, one person on the team that she sent us was a guy, so don't let the name of this organization limit you!

This Valentine's Day, turn your love outward and find a women's shelter in your community!

SHARING THE LOVE

Here are some ideas to help you and your friends bond with the kids at the shelter while sharing kindness and appreciation with those in your community. Sharing love feels as wonderful as receiving love.

This event can be thrown any time of year, but choosing a traditional holiday makes it extra festive. We decorate pumpkins with the shelter at Halloween and throw a huge Christmas party every year.

If you want to give the moms MANICURES, which I highly recommend, check out the Pre-Prom PhilanthroParty for nail art advice.

ALANNA WAS A HALO AWARD HONOREE WITH ME IN 2014!

CUPID'S CRAFTS

What You Need

- Colored or patterned paper (or both!)
- Markers, colored pencils, crayons, pens
- Stickers
- Scissors
- Glue
- Any other art supplies or decorative materials you have, other than glitter and a few more exceptions explained below.

How to Make It

Before heading to the shelter, meet with your volunteers to bake the sugar cookies, make sample valentine cards, and organize your supplies for fast and easy setup. Once you get there, invite the kids in the shelter to create personalized valentine cards. Encourage each to make two cards: a Valentine's Day card for their mom and an inspirational card for a kid in a nearby hospital. (If there isn't a children's hospital in your town, make valentines for senior citizens at a local home.) Teach the kids how to make do-it-yourself (DIY) heart envelopes (see page 28) to add a little extra love to their creations!

Here are two important notes: When you visit shelters and food banks, leave your cameras at home. Taking photos is not recommended and often not allowed. Also, when writing cards, remember to stay away from illness-related comments, such as "Get well soon" or "Feel better," because that's not a reality for some patients. Instead, offer the kids at the shelter a bunch of ideas for uplifting messages to use in their cards.

You are awesome
Never forget how amazing you are
You Rock
YOU SHINE BRIGHTER THAN THE SUN
You inspire me
YOU'RE SO BRAVE
I believe in YOU

And although I encourage you to embellish to your heart's content, leave the glitter at home. Since sequins and other loose decorations can be dangerous for kids' health (possible choking hazards), run your finger across the card; if nothing comes off, you're good to go. If you use stamps, double-check to make sure your stamp ink is dry before stacking the cards for delivery to the hospital. Place all of the cards in a large, 13 x 10 manila envelope for delivery. Individual envelopes are not necessary.

Since you won't know the names of the hospitalized kids who will be receiving the cards, use salutations like:

HEY THERE
Hey, you!
To a very special person
TO A ROCK STAR

FOOD FOR THOUGHT

Valentine cookies are a delicious staple treat of the holiday (right along with a box of chocolates). Make these simple no-chill cookies ahead of time and be sure to leave them undecorated. Pack some frosting, candy decorations, plastic knives, and a tablecloth for some messy, cookie decorating fun!

VALENTINE SUGAR COOKIES
{Makes 36 cookies}

What You Need
- 1 cup butter at room temperature
- 1½ cups granulated sugar
- 1 large egg
- 2 teaspoons vanilla extract
- 2¾ cups all-purpose flour
- 2 teaspoons baking soda
- 1 teaspoon salt
- Food coloring for frosting
- Large cookie cutters (preferably heart shaped)

How to Make It
1. Preheat oven to 350°F and line baking sheet with parchment paper.
2. Using a hand mixer, cream butter and sugar for about 4 minutes.
3. Blend in egg and vanilla.
4. In a separate bowl, combine flour, baking soda, and salt.

5. Add dry ingredients to mixer bowl and mix on low until a thick dough forms.

6. Divide the dough into two balls. Roll out each ball into a circle about ¼ inch thick. Use cookie cutters to shape.

7. Bake for 6 to 7 minutes or until the cookies are light brown around the edges. Move to cooling racks and cool completely before moving on to decorating.

8. Ready-made frosting will travel easier than homemade frosting. Buy white and mix it with different food colorings.

9. Bring a bunch of decorations to the party, like rainbow sprinkles, colored sugar, and chocolate chips.

TO MAKE COOKIE DECORATING EASIER, KEEP YOUR COOKIES ON THE THICKER AND LARGER SIDE. THIN SUGAR COOKIES TEND TO BREAK EASILY. THESE PLAYFUL COOKIES WERE DECORATED BY A SIX-YEAR-OLD GIRL AT THE DOMESTIC VIOLENCE SHELTER.

5

National Pancake Week: Flapjacks for Firefighters

FEBRUARY OR MARCH (DATES VARY)

HOST A PANCAKE BREAKFAST TO SUPPORT YOUR FIRE DEPARTMENT.

Contrary to popular belief, superheroes do exist. And your community is full of them. They may not have the ability to fly or shoot webs out of their wrists, but they're on the same mission as the caped heroes: to keep you safe. Police officers, paramedics, doctors, and firefighters all save lives every day, and that's pretty awesome. While some heroes play a more visible role in our lives, sometimes we forget about firefighters. Firefighters have a job that takes so much courage, and they deserve our recognition.

When I think of firefighters, I also think of pancakes. The Los Angeles Fire Department holds pancake breakfasts to support the firefighters, and I have memories of going to a few as a kid. These events always unite the community and give us a chance to meet and thank the people who risk their lives for ours.

Host your own neighborhood pancake breakfast to raise money for your local fire department. There's also a great charity called the National Fallen Firefighters Foundation that honors fallen firefighters and helps provide resources for their families. Invite neighbors and friends—including some local firefighters—to the celebration!

First off, contact your local firehouse station. Many fire stations have someone who works with community outreach, and that person can give you some ideas for how you can have firefighters participate in your event. On top of bringing your friends and members of your community together to celebrate these heroes (and feeding them, of course), you can coordinate with the station to make it an official fundraiser. Ask guests to bring a suggested donation (like $5 per person) to the event. Whether the funds raised go to the fire station for something they need or to one of the charities the fire station supports, your party will bring together the neighborhood to pay tribute to these heroes' dedication and hard work.

FIREFIGHTER "SURVIVAL KITS"[1]

Show your appreciation for firefighters in your area by assembling goody bags with your guests during your party and dropping them off at your local fire station after the party. Make sure to ask your local station how many firefighters and volunteers work there so each person will get one.

What You Need

- A printer and printer paper
- Decorative or normal scissors
- Glue sticks
- Brown paper lunch bags
- Art supplies
- Hole punch
- Red ribbon cut in 7-inch strips

Survival Kit
for Firemen

Life Saver
To remind you of the many times you've been one.

Starburst
For that burst of energy you'll need

Payday
Because you're not doing it for the money

Paper Clip
To help hold it all together

Hershey Kisses
Because you deserve them from all.

Gum
To help your unit stick together

Tootsie Roll
To help you roll with the punches.

Peppermint Patty

How to Make It

1. On a computer, type up this list of goodies and format it so that it is centered and prints out to a 5 x 7-inch size. Choose your favorite font, but make sure it's easy to read.

2. Print as many copies as you think you'll need, plus a couple extra, and cut out the lists using decorative or normal scissors.

   - Life Savers: Because that's what you are.

   - Starburst: Because you might need an extra burst of energy.

   - PayDay: Because you're not in it for the money.

   - Tootsie Roll: Because you need to roll with the punches.

   - Peppermint Pattie: Because keeping your cool under pressure can't be easy.

   - Snickers: Because a good laugh will keep your spirits up.

   - Mounds: Because it takes mounds of courage to do what you do.

   - Hershey's Kisses: Because there are not enough kisses in the world to thank you.

3. Glue a printout to the front of each bag. If you would like, set out a variety of craft supplies so your guests can decorate the goody bags.

4. Making sure the holes go through the front and back of each bag, punch one hole ½ inch from the top of the bag and ½ inch to the left of center. Punch another hole ½ inch from the top of the bag and ½ inch to the right of center.

5. Put one of each candy in every bag.

6. Lace the bag shut with a piece of ribbon. Tie with a neat knot or a bow so it faces the front of the "survival kit." Trim ends.

FOOD FOR THOUGHT

Pancakes seem like an obvious breakfast or morning party, but really pancakes are great at any time of the day. It all depends on what you top them with!

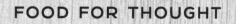

PANCAKES

{Makes about 15 pancakes. Multiply by number of attendees so there are plenty to go around. People will usually eat around 2 or 3 pancakes each.}

What You Need

- **4½ cups all-purpose flour**
- **3½ tablespoons baking powder**
- **3 teaspoons salt**
- **3 tablespoons granulated sugar**
- **4½ cups milk**
- **3 large eggs**
- **9 tablespoons butter, melted**

How to Make It

1. Heat a large nonstick pan on medium heat so that by the time you are ready to cook your pancakes, it will be nice and hot.

2. In a large bowl, gently whisk together all of the ingredients until the batter is moistened but still a tiny bit lumpy. (If you over-whisk, your pancakes will be too dense and flat.)

3. Using a ladle and working one at a time, scoop about ¾ cup of batter onto the hot nonstick pan.

4. When the edges are set, the top of the pancake is bubbly, and the bottom side is a deep golden brown (about 2 to 3 minutes), flip the pancake over and cook another 1 to 2 minutes. Transfer to a plate. Repeat until no batter is left. Pancakes are best served hot off the griddle, but to keep extras warm, place them on a cookie sheet in a 200 degree oven for up to 20 minutes.

TOPPINGS

Maple syrup and butter are traditionally served with pancakes, but how about surprising your guest with a range of topping options? Try some of these personal favorites!

Rocky Road: mini marshmallows and chocolate chips
Canadian Delight: maple syrup and crumbled bacon
Parfait: fruit, yogurt, granola, and honey
Teatime Treat: jam and clotted cream

6
Random Acts of Kindness Day: Smile-Gram PhilanthroParty

FEBRUARY 17

TO BOOST THE SELF-ESTEEM OF PEOPLE IN YOUR LIFE, WRITE KIND THOUGHTS ABOUT THEM.

One of Merriam-Webster's definitions of the word *philanthropy* is "goodwill to fellow members of the human race." While goodwill is definitely expressed through helping others in need, you can also show goodwill toward the people you encounter every day by telling family members how much you appreciate them, by helping a friend with homework, or by smiling at a stranger. I know, these small actions aren't typically considered philanthropic. However, kindness is at the core of philanthropy, and simply being a kind person is beneficial to you and those around you.

February 17 is Random Acts of Kindness Day. Gather a few of your friends and make compliment-grams to pass out at school. We teenagers tend to have a ton of insecurities, and receiving a thoughtful compliment is always a self-esteem boost. Try making compliment-grams for everyone in your grade, but if your grade is too big, make them for everyone in one of your classes. It's important to make sure nobody feels excluded. As an added bonus, this party works well for small gatherings and requires virtually no preparation. If you don't have the time or resources to throw a big event, you can still PhilanthroParty!

GOODWILL CRAFTING

Gather a few friends for an afternoon of kindness and crafts. This simple origami heart envelope is guaranteed to deliver smiles!

HEART ENVELOPES[2]

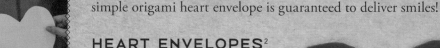

DON'T GET DISCOURAGED IF YOUR HEART ENVELOPE ISN'T PERFECT THE FIRST TIME. IT TAKES SOME PRACTICE, BUT YOU'LL GET THE HANG OF IT!

What You Need

- 1 sheet of colored or patterned paper (heavy paper or cardstock recommended)
- Pencil
- Scissors
- Stickers or glue stick
- Pens and markers

How to Make It

1. Begin with a sheet of colored or patterned paper. You may want to download and print a heart-shaped template and then trace it and cut it out. Or you can simply fold a paper in half, draw half of a heart along the crease, and cut it out for a symmetrical heart of your own design. You can write your compliment directly on the inside of the envelope or insert a separate compliment-gram later in the process.

2. Fold each side of the fancy heart about a third of the way in. Try to make the folds as straight and parallel as possible.

3. Insert your compliment. Fold down the top half of the heart to meet the center.

4. Finally, fold up the point of the heart. Flip it around and add your sticker. There's your envelope!

5. Write the recipient's name on the envelope flap and feel free to decorate with pens and markers!

How to Write a Compliment-Gram

1. Instead of writing general compliments for everyone, make each person feel special by being as specific as possible. What do you admire about that person? What makes them unique? Try to compliment character, not appearance. Think about what's on the inside!

2. Because you should be making compliment-grams for *everyone* in your grade or a certain class, it's likely that you'll come across somebody you don't know very well (or, let's just say it, maybe somebody you don't get along with). That's okay! You can still notice what's special about this person. Do they have good qualities that stick out? Maybe they're quiet but kind and observant, or maybe you've noticed they are talented at drawing or writing. As you practice writing nice things about people, you will discover that you can always find at least one nice thing to say about anyone, even those who aren't your favorites.

3. To make it even more personal, address your compliment-gram with the recipient's name and sign yours at the bottom.

IF THE COMPLIMENT-GRAMS ARE A SUCCESS, CONSIDER SETTING UP A TABLE AND SELLING COMPLIMENT-GRAMS AT SCHOOL FOR FIFTY CENTS AND DONATE THE PROCEEDS TO A CHARITY THAT WORKS TO PREVENT BULLYING, LIKE KIND CAMPAIGN OR WESTOPHATE. MAKE SURE YOU RUN THIS IDEA BY YOUR SCHOOL ADMINISTRATION FIRST, OF COURSE.

EXAMPLES OF COMPLIMENTS

You're a great listener.

You always know just what to say.

YOU SEEM TO REALLY KNOW WHO YOU ARE.

I know I can trust you.

YOU BRING OUT THE BEST IN OTHER PEOPLE.

You're so thoughtful.

I admire your [positivity, intelligence, generosity, confidence, or any other personality trait].

YOU INSPIRE ME.

YOU MAKE THOSE AROUND YOU FEEL COMFORTABLE.

MARCH

HERE ARE SOME MORE CELEBRATORY
THEMES FOR THE MONTH OF MARCH.

Nutrition Month

Women's History Month

Red Cross Month

Girl Scouts' Week—dates vary

National Bubble Week—dates vary

Popcorn Lovers' Day—date varies

Middle Name Pride Day—date varies

Incredible Kid Day—date varies

Daylight Saving (Time Change)—first Sunday in March

Old Stuff Day—March 2

Dentist's Day—March 6

Plant a Flower Day—March 12

National Pi Day—March 14

Extraterrestrial Abductions Day—March 20

Take a Walk in the Park Day—March 30

7

Music in Schools Month:
Music Matters Open Mic

HOST A CONCERT SUPPORTING MUSIC IN SCHOOLS.

I have always been a musician. I've never been good at sports. I was the *only* girl in my grade who wasn't on a sports team, and although we had singing classes a few times a week, the musicians didn't have the same facilities to develop our craft as the athletes. Our talents and commitment weren't as recognized by the school. Numerous studies have shown how music education enhances our overall ability to learn and actually *improves* academic performance.[1] But the importance of music in schools has been increasingly dismissed, and music programs are sadly undermined—frequently under threat of being cut—as budgets shrink.

Here's one way to work more music into your school: February is Music in Schools Month—the perfect opportunity to give musicians the spotlight by hosting an open mic night. Invite

your musically talented friends to perform, sell tickets for $5, and donate the proceeds to the school's music or arts program. Throw the party at your house or coordinate with your school to see if you can host it on campus. If your school music program needs some love, ask a member of the administration how your fundraiser can contribute. You could also do some research and connect with another school in your community that has a music program in need of support, or donate to an afterschool program that promotes the arts. Create a sense of occasion by using our guide to set up your own DIY stage and serve some music-themed treats.

THE SHOW MUST GO ON

Set up a small table by the door—run by either you or a volunteer—to collect "support the arts" donations as people come in. And set up a tip jar on stage in case anyone is inspired to give again! Have a signup sheet there where the open mic musicians can list their name, their instrument, the song they'll be performing, and a fun or weird fact about them that you can announce before each person goes up to perform. The open mic doesn't have to be limited to instrumental performance. You can also open up the stage to those who want to sing, perform some standup comedy, read poetry, or do a magic trick. Even a simple, well-rehearsed "Chopsticks" duet is fair game for this concert. Kids learning a new instrument should be especially welcome to perform in public for the very first time.

At the start of the show, get up on stage and tell guests about the cause they have donated to.

TIPS FOR OPEN MIC NIGHT

1. **Location.** Throwing this party at your house is highly encouraged! Clear the furniture out of your living room, garage, family room, or basement. If the weather is nice, set up in your backyard, and make sure you have access to electrical outlets. (Note: Check with your neighbors in advance since you may be creating some noise. You can also invite them!) If you don't think your house will work out, team up with a friend who's willing to host it at their house. Or see if your school or a local café is willing to host your party.

2. **Seating.** There are plenty of ways you can seat your guests using things you already have at home. Spread out blankets, pillows, and beanbags to create a chill and comfy atmosphere. Or gather all the chairs in your house and borrow some from friends.

3. **Stage.** You don't need an actual stage to have a successful open mic night. Just clear an area to use for performances. If you're outside, you'll most likely want to set up a platform or put down a rug so your performers don't have to set their

IF YOU AREN'T COMFORTABLE BEING THE MC (MASTER OF CEREMONIES), TALK WITH YOUR FRIENDS AND VOLUNTEERS TO FIND SOMEONE WHO IS COMFORTABLE WITH PUBLIC SPEAKING.

equipment on the grass. Provide a stool in case your performers prefer to sit, and place a pitcher of water and cups or glasses on a small table nearby.

4. **Decorations.** Make your stage look extra cool. Break out your Christmas lights or use lamps to light up the performance area. You can find specialty lights and lanterns, balloons, garlands, and more for cheap at a party store or a dollar store—everything you need to transform your space into an awesome event venue.

5. **Equipment.** You're going to need a microphone and amps to start with. If you don't have those, some of your guests probably do. Create a private Facebook group, make a Google doc, or send an email to your guests to coordinate equipment. Find out what people have and who's comfortable bringing in equipment to share. This is essential if you want the night to run smoothly.

6. **Tickets.** To inform your guests about the cause, print out tickets or programs with information about music in schools and the organization or school to which their donation is going.

I personally love tinsel decorations, and I think tinsel curtains make a great backdrop for a stage. Ask around and see if any of your friends or family have a stash of these glitzy curtains they will let you borrow. Or make use of what you already have at home and hang a sheet on a wall or fence as a simple backdrop.

FOOD FOR THOUGHT

Bake this funky Piano Key Cake for everyone to enjoy! With white frosting and Kit Kat bars, you can transform a delicious vanilla cake into edible piano keys that will have your guests singing with joy.

PIANO KEY CAKE
{Serves 15 to 18 people}

What You Need

- ½ cup unsalted butter at room temperature (plus 1 tablespoon to grease the pan)
- 2¼ cups all-purpose flour (plus 1 tablespoon to dust the pan)
- 2¼ teaspoons baking powder
- ¾ teaspoon baking soda
- ½ teaspoon salt
- 1 cup plus 2 tablespoons granulated sugar
- 3 large eggs
- 1 cup buttermilk
- 1½ teaspoons vanilla extract
- 27-inch-long piece of clean cardboard (make sure it's about 6 inches wide)
- Two 1-pound containers ready-made vanilla frosting or 4 cups homemade vanilla frosting (see Buttercream Frosting recipe on page 164)
- Black food coloring
- Pastry piping bag
- 36 Kit Kat bars, separated and cut in half

IF YOU DON'T HAVE A PASTRY PIPING BAG, THAT'S OKAY! PLACE THE FROSTING IN A STURDY PLASTIC SANDWICH BAG AND CUT A TINY HOLE IN ONE OF THE CORNERS. VOILA!

How to Make It

1. Preheat oven to 350°F.

2. Lightly butter a 9 x 13-inch baking pan. Lightly dust with extra flour, tapping out excess.

3. In a large bowl, whisk together flour, baking powder, baking soda, and salt.

4. With an electric mixer on high speed, beat butter and sugar until pale and fluffy, about 5 minutes. Beat in eggs, one at a time, until combined.

5. Reduce the mixer speed to low. Add flour mixture in three batches, alternating with two batches of buttermilk; beat to combine, scraping down sides of bowl as needed.

6. Beat in vanilla.

7. Transfer batter to prepared pan; smooth top with a spatula or knife.

8. Bake, rotating halfway through the baking time, until cake is golden and puffed and a toothpick comes out clean, about 30 minutes. Transfer from pan to a wire rack to cool completely.

9. Once cooled, cut the cake evenly down the center. Place each narrow cake section side by side onto the makeshift cardboard platter to make one long cake.

10. Measure 1 cup of frosting into a small bowl and add black food coloring (about 10 to 12 drops) until it is completely black.

Decorating

1. Spread the plain white vanilla frosting onto the cake, covering the seam between the two cakes so it appears seamless.

2. Facing the long edge of the cake, place the Kit Kat halves to look like black piano keys.

3. Finally, create the white keys of the piano by piping lines with the black frosting in a pattern resembling a piano keyboard.

8
Reading Month: Follow the Reader

HOST A BOOK CLUB PARTY AND BOOK DRIVE TO ENCOURAGE LITERACY IN YOUR COMMUNITY.

A good book is a powerful thing. It can transport you to a different time and space, make you laugh and cry, and maybe even change the way you see the world around you. It's a nice way to escape reality for a while. Reading has an amazing impact on your brain too! A study at Emory University found that becoming absorbed in a fiction book actually strengthens overall brain function.[2] And emotionally investing yourself in characters makes it easier to put yourself in another person's shoes in real life. Look at it this way: the tears you shed over Dumbledore's fate actually contributed to your ability to empathize. But the importance of literacy surpasses Harry Potter. Knowing how to read is a necessity.

Try to picture your life without reading or writing. Can you? According to UNICEF, nearly a billion people entered the twenty-first century without knowing how to read or even sign their names. And two-thirds of those people were women.[3] Illiteracy doesn't just mean people are missing out on great books; it's also linked to crime. The Department of Justice states that over 70 percent of inmates in American prisons can't read above a fourth-grade level.[4] Literacy is a human right, and it's essential to leading a complete life.

37

Lulu's Favorite Classics

THE LITTLE PRINCE

FRANNY AND ZOOEY

A TREE GROWS IN BROOKLYN

TO KILL A MOCKINGBIRD

ANNE OF GREEN GABLES

LORD OF THE FLIES

THE GIVER

THE CHRONICLES OF NARNIA (SERIES)

The problem may seem big, but there's a simple way to start a dialogue and encourage literacy in your community: host a book club. March is National Reading Month, so invite your friends to read a book with you and then get together and discuss your opinions. Ask members to bring in gently used books to donate. Explore schools in your town or state that may be in need of books or donate through organizations like Worldwide Book Drive or Milk + Bookies. When I was in elementary school, there was an underserved elementary school within walking distance from my school. My class collected books to stock their empty library. We also started a program in which we were each assigned a second-grade "reading buddy," and we walked to the school to read to them three times a year. At the end of the year, we gave our buddies books to take home. It was a really meaningful experience for the kids in my class and the kids we worked with. I encourage you to look for local schools to donate your books and time to as well.

Consider exploring nonfiction novels about social causes that pique your interest, although fiction is encouraged as well. For ideas, check out my list of favorites!

TURNING THE PAGE

Hosting a book club means you get to read a great book, hang out with your friends, and (my favorite part), chat about the book at length. With so many wonderful books out there and more being published every month, it can be daunting trying to pick a book for your party. One option is to narrow your search by choosing five of your favorite genres. Love creepy science-fiction novels or juicy teen romance books? How about biographies, self-help books, or nonfiction about real-life social activists? Do some research on classics and new releases in each genre. Then, consider including a voting ballot in your invitation with your top pick from each category so club members can have the final say. Send out invitations around a month in advance, so everyone has enough time to finish the book.

If your book club meeting is a success, why stop? Pick another book as a group and meet again next month! Book clubs are great motivation to stay on top of your reading, and it's always awesome having friends to discuss your opinions with.

DISCUSSION TOPICS[5]

Use these questions to help guide your conversation. Try to make sure everyone who wants to has a chance talk.

1. Talk about your experience reading the book. How did it make you feel? Did you have trouble putting it down at times, or did you find yourself bored?

2. Who are your favorite or least favorite characters? What are their personalities like, and what motivates them to act? What are their interactions with other characters like? How do these characters change by the end of the book?

3. What passages or quotes stood out? Why did these parts of the book resonate with you?

4. Did the book have a message or theme? Lots of books involve commentary about society. If there is, talk about it. What was the author critiquing? Were they effective in doing so?

5. How did you feel about the ending? Why did the author choose to end the book in that way? How would you change the ending if you could?

> Another DIY alternative is creating bookplates for your book donations. Simply use sticker labels and art supplies to write a message for the recipient, like *This Book Belongs to You* or *I Hope You Love This Book as Much as I Do*. Glue it on the book's inside cover and leave a space for the recipient to write their name.

DIY TASSLE BOOKMARKS

Make tassel bookmarks to put in your donated books. If you like, write inspirational quotes on the bookmark to encourage reading!

What You Need

One 6-strand skein of embroidery floss (8¾ yards)
Two 9-inch strands of embroidery floss or thin ribbon (⅛-inch wide)
Scissors
Cardstock, preferably scrapbook cardstock (double-sided design)
Hole punch
Glue stick
Art supplies of your choice: markers, glitter, patterned paper, etc.

INSPIRATIONAL READING QUOTES[6]

Once you learn to read, you will be forever free.
—FREDRICK DOUGLASS

The more that you read, the more things you will know. The more you learn, the more places you'll go.
—DR. SEUSS

To learn to read is to light the fire.
—VICTOR HUGO

There is more treasure in books than in all the pirates' loot on Treasure Island.
—WALT DISNEY

Reading is to the mind what exercise is to the body.
—JOSEPH ADDISON

A book is a dream that you hold in your hand.
—NEIL GAIMAN

Great books help you understand, and they help you feel understood.
—JOHN GREEN

Making the Tassel

1. Fold the skein of embroidery floss in half by bending it around your index finger at the halfway point, forming a loop.

2. Pull out your index finger and pinch the thread about 1 inch from the top of the loop.

3. Wrap one of the 9-inch pieces of thread or ribbon 6 or 7 times around the loop, directly above where you are pinching it.

4. There should be enough thread left hanging to tie into a tight double knot. Trim the knot's ends.

5. Evenly trim and fluff the fringe of your tassel.

Attaching the Tassel to your Bookmark

1. Cut cardstock into two 8 x 2-inch strips. Decorate these any way you want.

2. Punch a hole in the center of the 2-inch end, ½ inch down from the top edge.

3. Take the remaining piece of 9-inch embroidery floss or ribbon and thread it through the tassel's loop.

4. Tie the ends of the thread in a knot and trim it. This forms a loop that links to your tassel.

5. Pass the looped thread through the hole punched in your cardstock.

6. Pass the tassel through the loop that has been passed through the hole. Pull on the tassel.

9
Craft Month:
Art with a Heart

Being a teenager is filled with inner struggles. There's no escaping the confusion and anxiety of being stuck somewhere between childhood and the adult world, and I would be lying if I said I had it figured out. I do, however, have a single piece of wisdom that I guarantee will make your awkward in-between state a little less terrifying: keep a journal. Write down your thoughts and your fears and the things that make you happy. Put it all in there! Bad poetry, love letters, and angry rants are highly encouraged. It's also the perfect space for art-making of almost every medium. Journals are outlets for your personal self-expression, and nobody else ever has to see what you write and create.

I've been keeping journals throughout high school, and putting things down on the page always helps me to better understand what's going on in my head. I love making collages in my journals. I use whatever I can find: magazine cutouts, found photographs, receipts, old math tests, gum wrappers, Band-Aids—anything that conjures a memory or a feeling. Collaging is therapeutic, and the end product is always pretty cool. It's also a form of artistic expression that doesn't require skill or talent. If you have scissors and a glue stick, you are good to go! I look at my journals as private encyclopedias that document different phases of my life. Plus, when you're a gray-haired senior citizen reminiscing about the good ol' days, you'll have access to your teenage thoughts, which I think is the coolest thing ever.

March is National Craft Month (Reading *and* crafts? March *rocks*!), which means it's a perfect time for one of my all-time favorite PhilanthroParties: what I like to call the Art with a Heart Party. Invite

friends over to decorate their own journals. Ask guests to bring new art supplies with them to be donated to a local children's hospital or an art-based nonprofit or an under-served school. In Los Angeles, there's a great organization called Rainbow Pack that was founded by Riley Gantt when she was just ten years old. Riley fills backpacks with art and homework supplies and then delivers them to students in low-income districts. Many of the kids she serves cannot complete homework assignments and creative projects because they don't have necessary supplies at home. So let's spark creativity for kids in need and for guests at your party. Art supply donations are required; talent is optional!

THERE'S A PICASSO IN EVERYONE

This is Riley Gannt, founder of Rainbow Pack. We met when we were five years old at a kid's art studio run by her mom. We were reunited eleven years later when we both were asked to speak at a social action event.

At the heart of any successful party is planning and execution. To throw an Art with a Heart get-together, arrange all the crafting materials you'll need ahead of time. Invite guests to bring photos, memorabilia, or whatever artsy stuff sparks their imagination. Perhaps they would like to bring their own journals to personalize. Set up the ultimate journal-decorating table with all of the gathered art supplies and encourage everyone to create unique, meaningful collages on the covers of their journals.

BECAUSE JOURNALS CAN
GET A LITTLE PRICEY,
SPIRAL NOTEBOOKS OR
COMPOSITION BOOKS ARE
TERRIFIC SUBSTITUTIONS.
OR, ASK YOUR GUESTS
TO BRING IN THEIR OWN
BLANK BOOKS.

What You Need

Journals, composition books, or notebooks

Magazines

Newspapers

Vintage materials (old books, magazines, maps, sheet music,
found photographs)

Colored or patterned paper

Personal items like ticket stubs or meaningful scraps

Stickers

Colored markers, pens, or pencils

Tape

Glue

Mod Podge (glue sealer and finish) and foam brush
to apply (optional)

Tips for Collaging

1. Before your party, stop by a local flea market or
secondhand store and look for old magazines,
photographs, and other vintage treasures for your
collages.

2. Don't dismiss anything as junk. Your candy wrapper,
old math homework, or ticket stub could enhance your
collage!

ART SUPPLIES DONATIONS
HERE'S A LIST OF SUGGESTED
SUPPLIES THAT YOU CAN
SHARE WITH YOUR GUESTS
BEFOREHAND.

Construction paper
Plain or ruled paper
Markers
Crayons
Glue
Buttons
Fabric
Clay

ONE HOT SUNNY AFTERNOON IN THE MIDDLE OF THE OCEAN

3. Cut out letters or phrases from
   newspapers or magazines beforehand
   for your friends to use.

4. Stickers are highly encouraged!

5. While you can collage directly onto
   your journal or notebook, you might
   want to make a book cover instead. In
   that case, make sure you have plenty
   of craft paper and tape on deck.

6. Optional: Use Mod Podge to give
   your collage a glossy finish.

APRIL

ADDITIONAL APRIL EVENTS

HERE ARE SOME NATIONAL CELEBRATORY
THEMES FOR THE MONTH OF APRIL.

National Humor Month
International Guitar Month
Stress Awareness Month
Library Week—dates vary
Karaoke Week—dates vary
Tweed Day—April 3
World Health Day—April 7
Name Yourself Day—April 9
Siblings Day—April 10
Scrabble Day—April 13
International Moment of Laughter Day—April 14
National Cheeseball Day—April 17
Kindergarten Day—April 21
National Jelly Bean Day—April 22
Tell a Story Day—April 27
Honesty Day—April 30
Astronomy Day—dates vary, observed twice yearly
Dyngus Day—date varies, but always the Monday after Easter

10

April Fools' Day: Pranks for a Purpose

APRIL 1

ENJOY AN APRIL FOOLS' DAY-THEMED PARTY TO SPREAD KINDNESS.

My birthday is April 1. Yes, I'm an April Fool—literally. You'd expect that April Fools' Day would make a great birthday, and for most people I'm sure it would. You can play tricks on your friends, and they're not allowed to get mad because it's your special day! But I never quite caught on to the whole pranking thing. I thought the idea of tricking friends was mean, even if the tricks were totally harmless.

The year I turned eight, my parents asked if they could set up some small pranks for me and my friends to add some extra fun to my birthday sleepover, and I decided to give pranking a try. My parents set up pranks all over the party: rubber rats in the toes of our sleeping bags, powder that turned milk into goop for our breakfast cereal, a fake camera that squirted water, and a stink bomb for the car ride home after dinner. *Bon Voyage, Bob!* was written on the top of my birthday cake in pink frosting. But as my guests arrived, I panicked. I didn't want my friends to be scared or grossed out or have their feelings hurt because we were fooling them. So I decided to warn everyone. About everything. "Don't go in there—there's a stink bomb!" "Check your sleeping bags for rats!" You get the idea. My parents have never pulled a prank on me since that day.

What I didn't understand then was that the main element of a prank is the surprise factor. And even though pulling shocking or gross pranks can be fun, pleasantly surprising people is a different kind of fun, and it's rewarding for everyone involved. So regardless of whether or not it's your birthday, I encourage you to throw an April Fools' Day hangout that encourages both kinds of surprises.

PRANKING IT FORWARD

Whether it's buying coffee for the stranger behind you in line, cleaning the house *before* your parents have to ask, or telling someone in your life how important they are to you, doing the unexpected is a surefire way to brighten somebody's week. So why not throw an April Fools' Day party complete with both stink bombs *and* kindness? Stock your house with pranks and invite your friends over for fake bugs, whoopee cushions, and fake-out food. Then, put together goody bags that encourage your guests to get out there and and give someone a pleasant surprise!

GOOFY GOODY BAGS

Set up a goofy goody bag assembly table. Put together bags filled with gag gifts, treats, and a small prank-it-forward action that guests can do to surprise somebody in their community. You can do this either before the party or as an activity with your guests. When your friends leave, give them each a goody bag and set a one-week deadline for them to complete their purposeful prank. Request pictures for proof!

This PhilanthroParty is meant to spread kindness, but if you want to make it a fundraiser, throw a prank party on your birthday even if it doesn't fall in April. Ask for donations instead of presents and consider supporting a charity like Smile Train, in keeping with our theme of making people laugh. They provide surgery that gives children born with cleft palates the ability to eat, speak, and smile normally.

What You Need

- Gift bags or paper bags
- Paper
- Scissors
- Scotch tape or washi tape
- Pranks for a Purpose (see list)
- Post-It notes
- Small gag gifts (whoopee cushions, rubber chickens, etc.)
- Goodie bag fillers (party poppers, candy, cute socks, etc.)
- Tissue paper
- Stickers or other art supplies (optional)

How to Make It

1. Get a head count of the guests planning to come to your party and then buy the appropriate number of bags and fillers.

2. To add a little April Fools' charm to your goody bags, write jokes on tags and tie them to each bag.

3. If you'd like, use stickers or other art supplies to jazz up the outside of the bags.

4. Assemble your Pranks for a Purpose list. Check out ours for ideas. For each prank, attach a note explaining what your guest must do. Assemble one prank per guest. It's okay for multiple guests to receive the same pranks; as long as everyone takes home an action, you're good.

5. Set up a goody bag station: a pile of small gag gifts, a pile of Pranks for a Purpose (see below), and a pile of silly fillers you can buy at a local dollar store. Put one of each in each bag.

6. Finish off each bag by stuffing it with colorful tissue paper.

PRANKS FOR A PURPOSE
Here are some ideas for the purposeful party favors!

1. A small bag of change that the guest can use to fill someone's meter or leave at a playground to make a little kid's day

2. An apple to give to a teacher who inspires them

3. A blank thank-you card and a stamped envelope addressed to a local police or fire station

4. A coupon promising your parents one favor, such as a homemade meal or one day of chores

5. A coffee shop gift card (doesn't need to be more than $3) to buy coffee for the person behind you

6. A pack of flower seeds that you can plant to beautify a public space. Note: Check with your town's Parks and Recreation office to make sure it's okay for you and your guests to plant the seed packets around town. Also, make sure the flower seeds you will be using are native to your area.

7. A sponge to clean a parent's or neighbor's car

8. A pack of gum to give to a friend or sibling. It's a simple gesture but bound to brighten someone's day

9. A dog toy to drop off at a local shelter (Encourage your guests to spend some time with the animals!)

10. A small picture frame. (Tell your guests to frame a picture of them with their grandparents, parents, or friends and then send it to a person shown in the photo, along with a nice note.)

I put these super silly "Doughnut Seeds" in my goody bags. All you need is Cheerios and a plastic snack bag. Hopefully your gullible friends won't actually try to plant them!

FAKE-OUT FOOD

Fool your friends with these tricky treats. No one is prank-safe at this snack table! That delicious looking caramel apple may bring you to tears. That yummy Oreo cookie may have an odd, paste-like texture. Mix in a few caramel onions with the caramel apples. Replace the creamy center of a few Oreo cookies with toothpaste. Some guests will grab a delicious treat, and others may not be so lucky!

CARAMEL APPLES/ONIONS
{Makes 3 apples and 3 onions}

What You Need
- 6 craft sticks
- 3 medium apples
- 3 medium onions
- 14-ounce bag of caramels
- 1 tablespoon milk
- 1 buttered or wax-paper-lined baking sheet

MORE TRICKY
TREATS

1. Serve mashed potatoes in ice-cream cones.

2. Cook up some meatloaf or lasagna in pretty cupcake liners.

3. Sweet french fries and ketchup! Cut up some apples sticks with a crinkle cutter. Sprinkle on cinnamon and sugar and bake them for 8 to 12 minutes in a 400°F oven. Serve with a side of strawberry preserves.[1]

4. Take two pieces of sliced pound cake and add some yellow buttermilk frosting in between for a surprising "grilled cheese" treat.

5. Fill an empty doughnut box with a veggie platter.

How to Make It

1. Wash apples and remove stems.

2. Peel off dried layers of onions and trim ends.

3. Press craft sticks securely into the stem area of each apple and the trimmed end of each onion.

4. Unwrap caramels and place them in a microwave-safe bowl.

5. Add milk.

6. Microwave on high for 1 minute. Stir. Cook for 1 more minute or until caramels are melted and smooth.

7. Roll each apple and onion in the caramel and place stick side up on prepared baking sheet. Cool them in the fridge until the caramel has set.

Six of these are filled with toothpaste!

Which one is the onion?!

11

Earth Day: Guerilla Gardening PhilanthroParty

MAKE SEED BOMBS TO BEAUTIFY YOUR COMMUNITY.

No matter who you are or where you are from, you share a home with around 7 billion people. I think it's really cool that even though the human population is so diverse, we're all united by Mama Earth. But sadly, we earthlings are using up our resources, polluting the environment, causing the climate to change, and pretty much slowly destroying our world. Living in California, which is currently facing a severe drought, I've been watching the green slowly fade from my surroundings. Wildfires are devastating communities around the state. The agriculture industry, which uses around 80 percent of our water, is suffering and affecting the nation's food system as a whole. It has really brought to my attention the massive impact that humans have on our environment and the huge influence that the environment has on us.[2]

Every year on April 22, more than 192 countries unite to bring attention to problems facing our planet. Earth Day is a really important event, and a perfect opportunity to PhilanthroParty!

CAN YOU DIG IT?

Help increase greenery in your community by throwing a Guerilla Gardening Party and making your own all-natural DIY seed

Here's an eco-friendly tip: use seeds for green plants and flowers that are native to your area, like native wildflowers. They will be drought resistant and will need minimal maintenance, if any.

bombs! Plant them in a public area with permission or in your backyard. Private property is off-limits.

DIY SEED BOMBS[3]
{Makes about 30 seed bombs}

What You Need

- 8–10 packs of seeds or about ½ cup
- 5 cups cat litter (clean, of course, and bentonite based)
- 3 cups peat-free compost or potting soil
- 1 cup water
- Bowl
- Baking sheet
- Gloves

How to Make It

1. In a large bowl, combine seeds, cat litter, and compost.

2. Slowly add water while stirring the mixture with your gloved hands, until it feels like cookie dough.

3. Still with your gloves on, form cookie-sized balls (diameter of about 1 inch).

4. Dry the seed balls on a baking sheet in a sunny spot for at least 3 hours.

5. Once they are dry, leave them (or throw them!) anywhere, as long as they land on soil. Yup, you don't even have to plant them!

Where to Throw Seed Bombs

1. Vacant lots, abandoned side yards by the street, or any public areas that could use a little greenery

2. A local park, especially one that's been neglected

3. Your own backyard

BEES AND MONARCH BUTTERFLIES ARE ESSENTIAL POLLINATORS IN GRAVE DANGER, LARGELY BECAUSE PESTICIDES ARE DESTROYING THE MILKWEED AND WILDFLOWERS THEY DEPEND ON FOR SURVIVAL. DO SOME RESEARCH AND FIND OUT WHAT KINDS OF MILKWEED AND WILDFLOWERS ARE NATIVE TO YOUR AREA—AND USE THESE SEEDS FOR YOUR SEED BOMBS!

OOD FOR THOUGHT

Feed your hungry seed-bomb makers with—wait for it—dirt!
Make this easy, delicious Dirt Pudding for your guests to enjoy.

DIRT PUDDING
{Serves 12}

What You Need

- 3 boxes (3.9 ounces each) instant chocolate pudding mix
- 6 cups cold milk
- 12 Oreos or other hard chocolate wafer cookies
- Gummy worms or other gummy insects (optional)
- 12 small (8-ounce) mason jars or clean, unused mini terra cotta pots

How to Make It

1. Prepare the chocolate pudding according to the directions on the box. Make sure you do it early enough that it has time to chill before your party.

2. Place cookies in a plastic baggie and crush using a rolling pin or heavy jar until they look like dirt.

3. Spoon about ½ cup of pudding into each mason jar and top with crushed Oreos. If you like, garnish with your choice of gummy worms or gummy insects.

If you are serving your Dirt Pudding in a mini terra cotta or glazed flowerpot, make sure it is brand-new and has been washed. Plug the water drainage hole (if there is one) with a large marshmallow. Pour the pudding into the pot, top it off with crushed Oreos, and garnish with insect gummies or even chocolate rocks. Plant some tissue-paper blossoms (see the flower DIY on page 61) or fool the eye with a cheerful plastic flower growing right out of the oh-so-tasty dirt.

12
Poetry Month: Secret Poets' Society

SHARE POETRY IN UNEXPECTED WAYS.

SPRING IS HERE AT LAST, GOOD-BYE TO WINTER SNOW,
FLOWERS AND GREEN GRASS AND LEAVES BEGIN TO GROW.
TIME TO GRAB A PEN AND SIT UNDER A TREE,
'CAUSE IT'S APRIL AGAIN, THE MONTH OF POETRY!

What do you think of my poem? I wrote it to celebrate my favorite month. I love April, mainly because it's my birthday month, but also because it's National Poetry Month. April means it's time to whip up some metaphors, brush off your iambic pentameter, and plant the seeds of poetry in the hearts and minds of everyone! People tend to shy away from poetry, but it can be a really effective way to express yourself to the world from a uniquely personal angle. All you need to do is think about something that makes you feel things and then put those feelings into words. They can be beautiful, happy, wonderful feelings, or they can be ugly, dark, gloomy feelings. All feelings are valid! Your poem doesn't even have to rhyme if you don't want it to.

Poetry can be the most powerful way to vent, enlighten, disrupt, and release ideas and feelings that might be unhealthy to keep inside. For many at-risk youth in the inner city, this kind of expression is especially important, and yet their access to poetry and literary arts is limited. I am obsessed with the amazing work that comes out of an organization called Get Lit—Words Ignite. They

offer poetry classes and a platform for inner-city poets to write and be heard. So I came up with these PhilanthroParty ideas to support them and to share my love of poetry with my friends and community. Invite guests to attend a Secret Poets' Society Party at your house or participate in this Poet-Tree project!

SECRET POETS' SOCIETY PARTY

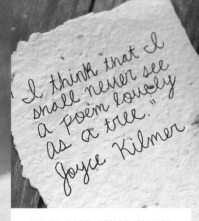

So what's the *secret* part in a Secret Poets' Society? Why, it's in the stealthy way you and your guests will use poetry to spread enlightenment and feel-good vibes in unexpected places!

Ask your guests to write or research short, uplifting poems, favorite song lyrics, or inspirational quotes and bring them to your party to copy onto small pieces of bioseed paper (see DIY on next page). Then take the party on the road! Go to a mall and discreetly leave your hopeful snippets on food court tables and dressing room chairs. Tape them to bathroom mirrors or drop them into tip jars. This goodwill PhilanthroParty gives your friends an opportunity to unleash their inner poets while brightening a stranger's day. As an added bonus, you'll be surprised how giddy (and sneaky!) you will feel while trying to leave the poems without being noticed. But be mindful that leaving poems behind could be considered littering, unless they are written on biodegradable paper. Check out this bioseed paper DIY and list of sample poems to get your Secret Poets' Society Party going!

POET-TREE PROJECT

For a traditionally philanthropic PhilanthroParty, consider partnering with a local café, bookstore, school, or organization—any supervised area where donations can be accepted. In honor of poetry month, ask them if they would display your Poet-Tree and accept donations to the Get Lit—Words Ignite organization for the entire month of April.

To make a Poet-Tree get together with friends to write out short poems on small cards. Place them in envelopes. On your computer, design stickers saying, *Pick a Poem* (or write them by hand) to place on the envelopes. Hang your poems on the branches of a small, portable tree. Put out a donation box and a sign instructing customers and passersby to pick a poem and then make a donation.

BIOSEED PAPER

Write your poems, lyrics, or quotes on this DIY seed paper so you don't create waste or litter. In addition to being inspired by the words written on this handmade paper, whoever finds your note can actually *plant* it! This DIY makes about ten sheets of paper, depending on their thickness.

What You Need

2 identical 5 x 7-inch wooden picture frames

Fine mesh screen cut to the size of the frames' outside edges

Staple gun

4 cups of shredded, used paper (avoid glossy and newsprint)

Blender

Strainer (kitchen colander)

Sink or basin (larger than your frame)

Packet of seeds (flat, noninvasive seeds work best, like tomato or poppy seeds)

10 absorbent cloths or paper towels (at least 5 x 7 inches each)

Sponge

Used newspapers

2 baking sheets

Heavy book or other object

How to Make It

1. Staple the screen to the back of 1 wooden frame to make the mold. Keep the second empty frame as is.

2. Soak 4 cups of shredded paper in warm water for at least 30 minutes.

3. Place a handful of soaked paper in blender. Add water until blender is ¾ full and then blend for about 30 seconds, until a soupy slurry is formed.

4. Pour the slurry into a strainer where it can drain.

5. Working in batches, repeat steps 3 to 4 until you have used all the soaked paper and have about 1 to 2 cups of pulp within the strainer.

LULU'S FAVORITE INSPIRATIONAL QUOTES

Remember to play after every storm.
—MATTIE J. T. STEPANEK

The sun is up; the sky is blue/it's beautiful, and so are you.
—JOHN LENNON AND PAUL MCCARTNEY,
"DEAR PRUDENCE" BY THE BEATLES

Forever—is composed of Nows.
—EMILY DICKINSON

The worst enemy to creativity is self-doubt.
—SYLVIA PLATH

*There is nothing noble in being superior to your fellow man;
true nobility is being superior to your former self.*
—ERNEST HEMINGWAY

*It is only with the heart that one can see rightly;
what is essential is invisible to the eye.*
—ANTOINE DE SAINT-EXUPÉRY

6. Fill your sink or a basin about ½ full with water. Add seeds and 1 to 2 cups of pulp, depending on your desired paper thickness (use more pulp for thicker paper).

7. Place empty frame on *top* of the *screen* side of the mold and hold it together securely. Swirl the slurry to make sure the pulp hasn't settled. In one smooth motion, dunk both frames into the water and then lift the mold straight up out of the water.

8. Drain the water from the mold over the sink or basin, gently tilting the mold back and forth. Then, carefully lift off the top frame from one end first. The wet paper will stay on the screen.

9. Lay the mold screen side down onto a cloth (or paper towel) so the paper is directly on the cloth.

IMPORTANT NOTE!
This craft takes around 48 hours to do, so you'll need to make the bioseed paper prior to your guests' arrival to the Secret Poets' Society Party.

WHERE TO LEAVE YOUR POEMS

1. Inside library books
2. On windshields of parked cars
3. Inside tip jars (with monetary tip too!)
4. Under condiment jars on restaurant tables
5. On a seat at a food court

10. With the paper remaining under the mold screen, take the sponge and gently press as much water off the paper through the screen. Repeat until as dry as possible.

11. Lift off the mold. If the paper sticks gently peel it off the mold from the corners. Once lifted, place another absorbent cloth on top of the paper. Press down firmly with the sponge on the cloth to absorb more water.

12. Repeat steps 1 to 10, separating each sheet of paper with an absorbent cloth.

13. Place a final absorbent cloth on top of your stack and move the stack to a baking sheet lined with a small pile of newspapers. Place the second baking sheet on top of the stack and weigh it down with a large book or a heavy object.

14. Leave the sheets to press for 30 minutes. Carefully separate each absorbent cloth with paper attached. Spread them out and let each paper dry on top of its cloth for several hours. Optional: When they are totally dry, you may want to iron the paper for a smoother finish or press them under heavy books again.

15. Write a poem, lyric, or quote on the unseeded side, and encourage the finder to plant your creation. Add these planting tips to the paper:

    PLANT ME! This poem is brought to you on bioseed paper. Cover me with a small layer of soil and water lightly. Keep soil wet until the seeds sprout.

MAY

ADDITIONAL MAY EVENTS

HERE ARE SOME MORE NATIONAL CELEBRATORY
THEMES FOR THE MONTH OF MAY.

National Barbecue Month
National Bike Month
National Hamburger Month
National Teacher Appreciation Day—Tuesday of the first full week in May
Space Day—first Friday in May
Mothers' Day—second Sunday in May
Brother and Sister Day—May 2
Cinco de Mayo—May 5
Lost Sock Memorial Day—May 9
Clean up Your Room Day—May 10
Chocolate Chip Day—May 15
Love a Tree Day—May 16
Wear Purple for Peace Day—May 16
International Museum Day—May 18
National Missing Children's Day—May 25
Water a Flower Day—May 30
World No-Tobacco Day—May 31

13
May Day:
Spring into Action

MAY 1

CREATE CHEERFUL BASKETS FOR SENIORS.

or years, every time May 1st rolled around I heard people talking about May Day and never knew what it meant. I decided to do some research on this mysterious holiday, and this is what I found out: May Day really has no single definition. Different cultures celebrate May 1 in different ways. In England, Germany, and Sweden, it's a traditional celebration of spring, where people gather around a Maypole and dance, sing songs, and eat cake. In Eastern European countries, May Day is celebrated as Labor Day or seen as a day for political action. Of the May Day traditions I came across, my favorite was an American one, in which people filled "May baskets" with flowers and other goodies and hung them on the door of someone they cared about.

How cool would it be if we still did that? The good news is, we can! Bring back the tradition this May Day with a PhilanthroParty that spreads spring cheer to a local senior center.

APRIL SHOWERS BRING MAY FLOWERS

Invite friends over to make May Day baskets for senior citizens. Set up a craft table with all the basket materials and use my easy DIY guide to make gorgeous paper flowers to put inside. Why paper flowers? Because they will continue to cheer up a senior's room long after real flowers wilt and die. They don't need watering, and I can't think of a single soul who is allergic to tissue paper! These are important factors to consider when you're planning your gifts. I also like to wrap up a few small thoughtful gifts in my May baskets.

Well in advance, pick a local retirement home in your community and call to inquire about any guidelines they might have and how many baskets you may need for their residents (you don't want to leave anyone out!). Then go ahead and schedule the visit. Once you and your friends have crafted your May Day baskets, take a field trip to deliver them to the retirement home. In the spirit of May Day traditions, you might also bake a cake for the celebration (check out the Vanilla Cake recipe on page 35—just omit the piano decorations).

PAPER FLOWERS

What You Need
    A few packs of tissue paper in different colors
    Dental floss, floral wire, or string
    Scissors

How to Make It

1. Most tissue paper is 20 x 30 inches. Depending on what size flower you want, cut the tissue paper into quarters or eighths by folding it and cutting along the creases.

2. Lay 4 to 6 sheets of tissue directly on top of each other (4 sheets for smaller flowers, 6 for larger ones). Starting at one end, accordion-fold the paper all the way across, creasing with each fold.

3. Cut a convex, half-moon shape at either end of the folded strip, rounding out the edges.

4. Wrap floral wire, dental floss, or string around the center of the folded strip, and twist or tie a knot to hold the folds together.

5. Fan out the accordion folds in a circle and begin to pull each layer of tissue paper away from the center, one at a time.

6. Ta-da! You have a paper flower.

MAY BASKETS

Assembling DIY May Baskets

1. **Baskets.** Since it's early May, you can probably pick up some Easter baskets at your local craft, department, or dollar store. (If Easter has passed, maybe there will be a discount!) But don't feel limited to baskets: colored buckets and decorated shoeboxes are great alternatives. If you want to take a classic route, traditional May baskets were actually paper cones. Simply take a sheet of patterned paper (scrapbook paper is perfect), form a cone shape, staple on both ends, and fill it with paper flowers and goodies.

2. **What to put inside.** Check out this list of goodies to include in your May baskets for seniors. You can find everything you need at a dollar store or a drugstore.

3. **Flowers.** Finish them off with some lovely paper flowers.

May Basket Goodies

HERE ARE SOME CUTE AND PRACTICAL GIFTS
TO PUT IN YOUR MAY BASKETS!

Book of crosswords, word searches, or other puzzles

Mini-jigsaw puzzle

Teabags and packets of sugar or sweetener

Lotion or hand cream

Socks

Notepad and pen

Scented hand soap or sanitizer gel

Snacks such as popcorn, granola bars,
    or applesauce pouches

Treats such as chocolate, lollipops, or cookies

MAYPOLE CAKE

This super-simple cake is meant to replicate a traditional Maypole still used for a ritual spring dance in many parts of America, England, and Sweden. In fact, my school erects a giant Maypole every May 1, and the sixth-grade girls learn the Maypole dance. For this cake, I plopped a few cupcakes on top of a layer cake. I stuck a kabob skewer in the middle and trailed ribbon from the top of the skewer down to each cupcake.

14
Pre-Prom PhilanthroParty:
The Cinderella Effect

COLLECT PROM DRESSES TO MAKE SOMEONE'S DREAM COME TRUE.

A highlight of my middle school experience was finally being old enough to go to school dances. I spent all of elementary school longing for the day when I would get to shop for a cute dress and dance on the assembly hall's linoleum floor. I have to admit that the dances never quite lived up to the hype. The best part was getting ready for the big night with my girlfriends. We'd meet at someone's house, order pizza, and blast our favorite music. We'd cram into the bathroom and talk about who we hoped to dance with as we put on mascara and did our hair. These will always be my favorite memories of school dances: hanging out with my friends beforehand and anticipating what was to come.

Writing this as a junior in high school, I'm excited to go to my first prom this year! Prom is such a high school milestone, and everyone should be able to feel their best and have a good time. But dresses can get very pricey, and this puts a big strain on many families. Luckily, organizations like Becca's Closet, Polished Girlz, and the Cinderella Project collect prom dresses to give to girls who might not have a dress to wear to prom.

Why not turn your pre-prom hangout into a Pre-Prom PhilanthroParty? Have your friends bring dresses that don't fit them anymore and then donate them. Even if your dance or prom takes place at the end of the season, someone will use them next year.

It seems like every time I look in my closet I find dresses that I've outgrown, dresses that could make another girl's prom experience extra special. May is typically prom season, but this event can be done for any school dance. Music and food must be included in your party, of course. Check out our snack ideas and prom pump-up playlist.

FAIRY GODMOTHER TIME!

Even Cinderella ends up with a beautiful "donated" gown in the fairy tale, and now you and your friends get a chance to play fairy godmother for other girls! Remember that the dresses you and your guests collect must be in good condition. Remind your friends to look over their dresses to ensure there are no holes, tears, stains, or odors.

To set the right atmosphere, you'll want space to primp. Clear off your bathroom counter and borrow as many mirrors as possible (even ask your guests to bring some). Set them up with good lighting and ask your parents if you can move lamps into the party space if necessary.

NAIL ART
Check out these easy DIY tips for glamorous prom nails.

What You Need
- 2 colors of nail polish
- Metallic Sharpie pens
- Bobby pins
- Scotch tape
- Clear topcoat polish (or a glitter topcoat)

How to Do It
1. Paint your nails using your first color. When they are completely dry, pick one of these fun designs.

   - **Gold Sharpie:** Add a golden French tip with a Sharpie to any solid-color manicure for a touch of glitz. Sharpie comes off easily with nail polish remover, and it's safe to use on your nails.

Lulu's Prom Playlist

"Girls Just Want to Have Fun" (Cyndi Lauper)

"Let's Dance" (David Bowie)

"Like a Prayer" (Madonna)

"P. Y. T. (Pretty Young Thing)" (Michael Jackson)

"Boys Don't Cry" (The Cure)

"Sweet Jane" (The Velvet Underground)

"Disorder" (Joy Division)

"Always Be My Baby" (Mariah Carey)

"Crazy in Love" (Beyoncé & Jay Z)

"Dancing on My Own" (Robyn)

"How Will I Know" (Whitney Houston)

- **Polka Dots:** Dip the circular end of a bobby pin into your second color and dab onto your nails for polka dots. You can put dots all over your nails, or just do a line around the edges.

- **Glittery Glam:** Add a topcoat of glitter polish to the top half of your nails for a gradual intensity.

- **Scotch Tape:** Scotch tape is your best friend when it comes to DIY nail art. Place a piece of tape diagonally across your nail and paint with a second coat for a half-and-half look. Or, place three very thin pieces of tape horizontally across your nail for stripes.

2. Once the second color dries, finish your nails off with a clear topcoat to prevent chipping.

PARTY MOCKTAILS

You and your guests may get pretty parched while gabbing and primping for the big dance. Offer this ice-cold pink treat.

VIRGIN FROZEN STRAWBERRY MARGARITAS
{Makes 4 servings}

What You Need
- 6 cups ice
- 1 can (12 ounces) frozen lemonade or limeade concentrate
- 1 cup frozen strawberries
- 1 cup lemonade or other fruit juice
- Sugar for glass rims

How to Make It

1. Place ice in a blender and crush for 10 to 20 seconds. Add the frozen lemonade concentrate, strawberries, and lemonade or juice. Blend until smooth.

2. Pour sugar into a flat bowl or plate. Dampen the rims of four glasses. Dip the edges of the glasses into the sugar.

3. Fill glasses with margarita mixture and serve cold.

15

Memorial Day:
Old-Fashioned Field Day Fun

PLAN A BARBECUE FOR A BETTER WORLD.

My mom has a good friend named Wendy. After a skiing accident, Wendy lost the ability to use her legs and now needs to use a wheelchair to get around. But Jasper and I have never thought of Wendy as "our mom's friend in a wheelchair." We've always thought of her as our mom's tennis partner. They used to rally regularly until Wendy's skill level outpaced my mom's, and she eventually became a US Open champion on the adaptive sports circuit. Wendy was able to continue her athletics after her accident through the help of some adaptive sports organizations. They support and empower people with physical and cognitive disabil-

ities and chronic illnesses by teaching them how to play sports regardless of their conditions. Learning how to play sports after her accident was crucial in Wendy's physical and mental healing process, as is the case for so many others in similar situations.

Along with being an amazing tennis player, Wendy's also on a basketball team with other paraplegics (people who can't use their legs). Jasper has always been particularly amazed by Wendy's athletic abilities. For his birthday one year, he threw a joint PhilanthroParty with his friend Jack, and instead of gifts they asked for donations to raise money for Wendy's basketball team.

Jasper and Jack rallied their fourth-grade class to volunteer at one of the basketball tournaments. The team ended up visiting his class and sharing the profound impact that sports and regular physical activity has had on their lives.

Seeing how important sports are to Wendy inspired me to do some research. I learned about the Adaptive Sports Foundation (ASF), an amazing organization with projects such as their nationally recognized Warriors in Motion program that helps troops injured in conflict gain an understanding of wellness and healthful living. To raise money for ASF, celebrate Memorial Day with your family by hosting your very own Field Day Tournament! And in the spirit of our national holiday, make it a barbecue.

FIELD OF DREAMS MEMORIAL DAY

Hosting a barbecue is a perfect opportunity to have your guests be part of determining the party menu. Decide with your family what things you want to provide and what you'd like to ask guests to bring (along with their financial donation for ASF, of course!). For example, you might provide the main courses—like hotdogs and burgers—and drinks. Then invite your guests to bring whatever they want to go with the grilled foods, from side salads to chips to desserts. Anything goes, but if you are inviting a lot of people, you may want to indicate who's bringing what, so you don't get lots of one thing!

If you can't host it in a backyard, try hosting it in a park. Find out if grilling is allowed and if there is a water source. If you can't fire up the grill, check out page 77 for eco-friendly suggestions for finger food!

FIELD GAMES

Next up is the entertainment. Since this party is all about encouraging physical activity, why not host a series of field games? Use my list of games to get you started and follow my instructions to create your own DIY ring toss.

Decide how you want to divide into teams and then come up with fun team names. Keep score by setting out markers and an easel pad or a big piece of white paper near the action. Write down each team's name

YOU CAN DIVIDE
INTO TEAMS IN
DIFFERENT WAYS:
BY FAMILIES, KIDS
VERSUS ADULTS,
OR BOYS VERSUS
GIRLS.

and, as they win points throughout the day, have them draw tally marks next to their names on the scoreboard. Set up a prize table for the winners. First-place team gets first choice of the prizes, second-place team chooses next, and so on.

DIY RING TOSS[1]

What You Need

9 empty 12-ounce glass soda bottles

Red, white, and blue fluid acrylic paint (or any three colors of your choice)

Six 3-inch plastic embroidery hoops

Red, white, and blue yarn or ribbon (must be same colors as paint)

Hot-glue gun

Rope or long stick

Scissors

How to Make It

1. Remove labels from glass soda bottles. (If they're stubborn, try soaking them in water or using Goo Gone.)

2. Pour 1 tablespoon of paint into a soda bottle. Roll the bottle to distribute the paint evenly inside. Turn it upside down onto a paper bag to allow excess paint to drip out. Stand it upright to dry.

3. Repeat step 2 for all bottles, painting 3 bottles red, 3 white, and 3 blue.

4. Loosen the screw on an embroidery hoop and discard the outer ring. Apply a dab of hot glue to the outside of the inner ring. Attach a piece of yarn or ribbon and wrap it around the hoop until the hoop is completely covered. Secure the end of the yarn or ribbon with another dab of hot glue and then trim away any excess.

5. Repeat step 4 for all embroidery hoops. End up with 2 red rings, 2 white, and 2 blue.

6. Once the bottles are dry, set them on your lawn or on a table. Determine where the player should stand and mark it with a rope or a stick. Each player gets 6 rings per turn. If their hoop lands on any bottle, that's one point. If it lands on a bottle of the same color, that's two points!

EVEN MORE FIELD DAY GAMES

Plan your party in a large yard or a public or school park with a grassy area big enough for races. Boundaries can be indicated with a stripe of flour, rope, or whatever else you have handy. Here are some other games that have stood the test of time.

1. *Egg and Spoon Relay Race:* Mark out a course for your race. If you have a lot of people, make it a relay, with meeting places ("exchanges") along the course. Starters line up on the starting line with an egg carefully balanced on a teaspoon or tablespoon and then fast-walk to the first exchange, where they carefully pass the egg to the next player. See who can reach the finish line first with their egg still intact.

In order to make sure things run smoothly, recruit volunteers to help you run the field day games. Make sure somebody's collecting donations by the door. As an additional option, I set out a used cell phone collection box every year for this party and for Fourth of July parties. Then, I donate the phones to an organization called Cell Phones for Soldiers that provides free communication services to troops and veterans. I have been reusing my box for years!

2. *Lawn Twister:* We are lucky to have a cotton picnic blanket that doubles as a twister board. If you have the actual game, you may find the plastic game mat too slippery on the grass. If that's the case, consider spray-painting the twister circles in the grass with sports chalk or paint.

3. *Potato Sack Race:* Heavy-duty trash bags work too—just be sure that young children are supervised and never put them over their heads.

4. *Water Balloon Toss:* Stand across from your partner and toss a water-filled balloon back and forth, taking a step backward away from each other after every catch. The last team still dry and standing wins.

5. *Three-Legged Race:* Tie your left leg to your partner's right (or vice versa) with a scarf or piece of fabric and race other teams to the finish line.

6. *Hula Hoop Contest:* Challenge others to see who can keep the hoop off the ground the longest.

7. *Watermelon Seed–Spitting Contest:* It's just what it sounds like! Line up, take a big bite of watermelon, and see who can spit their seeds the farthest. Flat surfaces like concrete or paved driveways are the best locations for this, since it's easier to see the seeds. (Remember to clean up afterward with a broom and a water hose.)

8. *Lawn Tic-Tac-Toe:* On your patio, draw a 3 x 3-foot tic-tac-toe board in chalk or spray-paint the board on your lawn. Get 10 beanbags or Frisbees from a dollar store, and mark 5 with X and 5 with O. Two people can compete, or one person can play solo.

People Who Inspire Lulu

These are some people who truly inspire me: creative thinkers who use their talents and wisdom as tools for lasting change. I'm drawn to quite a few people who share my love of music and art and have figured out how to turn their passions and talents into platforms for social good.

MATTIE J. T. STEPANEK

Mattie J. T. Stepanek was a poet and peacemaker. Before he died at age thirteen, Mattie's simple poems brought hope to a nation that was suffering after 9/11. His work gained the attention of kings and presidents, and he was even a favorite guest of Oprah Winfrey, who helped his books become *New York Times* best sellers. He woke up the world to the power and relevance of what young people have to say and what they can accomplish. Mattie paved the way for this generation of youth activists. Because of him, I grew up in a world where people were willing to give me a chance to create change.

KATHLEEN HANNA

Kathleen Hanna is a punk rock artist and feminist icon. As the lead singer of Bikini Kill and Le Tigre, Kathleen used her music to create the influential third-wave feminist riot grrrl movement, which promotes female empowerment and encourages women to express themselves through music.

JENA NARDELLA

Jena Nardella is an activist and music lover. At age twenty-one, Jena approached her favorite Grammy Award–winning band, Jars of Clay, about using their music as a platform to bring clean water and HIV medical support to the most remote areas of Africa. Together they founded the organization Blood:Water (page 117) and helped a million people in their first ten years. Jena was one of the first people outside my family to genuinely believe in me and teach me valuable lessons about responsible and sustainable giving.

MALALA YOUSAFZAI

Malala Yousafzai is an advocate for girls' education and the youngest Nobel Peace Prize laureate to date. She became an activist when she was just eleven years old, writing a blog for the BBC, and since then has become one of the most power-

ful voices fighting for education equality. She's hands-down the coolest and bravest girl on the planet. Check out her organiza-tion, the Malala Fund, to keep up-to-date on education issues and to support her cause.

NILE RODGERS

Nile Rodgers is a legendary musician and philanthropist. Whether or not you're aware of it, you have definitely danced and sung along to Nile Rodgers's music. Nile is a founding member of the disco band Chic, who released smash hits such as "Le Freak" and "Good Times," and has worked with art-ists such as Madonna, David Bowie, Michael Jackson, Daft Punk, Lady Gaga, Sam Smith . . . The list goes on! Nile was also behind the song "We Are Family," and after 9/11, he founded the We Are Family Foundation, which gives a platform to young change-makers with visions of a better world. I had the honor of attending the We Are Family Foundation's program called Three Dot Dash when I was twelve years old, where I met Nile and had one of the most incredible and inspiring experiences of my life.

JUNE

ADDITIONAL JUNE EVENTS

HERE ARE SOME MORE NATIONAL CELEBRATORY
THEMES FOR THE MONTH OF JUNE.

Aquarium Month
Candy Month
Dairy Month
National Fresh Fruit and Vegetables Month
Garden Week—dates vary
Doughnut Day—first Friday in June
Father's Day—third Sunday in June
International Children's Day—varies by country, but widely June 1
Repeat Day—June 3
Best Friends Day—June 8
Flag Day—June 14
International Yoga Day—June 21
Solstice—date varies, but most often June 21
National Pink Day—June 23
Forgiveness Day—June 26

16

International Picnic Day:
A Day in the Park

JUNE 18

MAKE SANDWICHES FOR THE HOMELESS, CLEAN UP THE PARK, AND PICNIC WITH FRIENDS.

I often forget how nice it is to go outside. Due to mountains of homework and the invention of Netflix, I spend a lot of time in my bedroom. But whenever I do get outside, whether it's running around in my backyard, taking my dog on a walk, or hiking with my mom, I feel so invigorated that I wonder why I don't do it more often.

Because a true outdoor lifestyle isn't always an option for us urban dwellers, our parks become our lifeline to the peace and serenity that only nature can provide. So I have to wonder why picnics seem to have become lost pastimes. If you ask me, it doesn't get much better than eating food and enjoying nature in the company of your friends. I think it's time to bring picnics back and start a revolution!

June 18 is International Picnic Day, the perfect launch date. Gather your friends at your house, make sandwiches and other snacks, and go spend some time outside at a local park. All revolutions have some social good involved, right? So clean up the park before you have your picnic (a community steward is someone who leaves a public space cleaner than how they found it) and make extra sandwiches for anyone you see who looks like they haven't had a good meal in a while. Follow our tips on how to handle food safely and stay eco-friendly. Happy picnicking!

PREPARING YOUR PERFECT PICNIC

If you're like me, your picnic skills are probably a little rusty. Here's a basic checklist to make sure you're fully prepared to clean up the park and then have a relaxing picnic with your friends.

Picnic basket or bag: Find one with insulation to keep items cool or bring a cooler.

Blanket: Bring one that is washable and that you're not afraid to get dirty.

Food: Try to reduce waste by packing finger food.

Plenty of water: Freeze bottles of individual drinks the night before to double as ice for your cooler or picnic basket.

Trash bags: Bring one color for recycling and another color for trash.

Work gloves: Try dollar stores and any stores with a garden center.

Extra sandwiches to give to the homeless that you might encounter at the park: If you don't give away all your prepared sandwiches, drop them off at a church or organization that distributes fresh food donations.

CLEAN UP KIT

SAFE SANDWICHES!

Bacteria forms in two hours with most meats and cheeses when they're unrefrigerated, so when packing sandwiches to donate, use ingredients that can go six hours without refrigeration:

SWEET: NUT BUTTERS, JAMS, BANANAS, HONEY

SAVORY: HUMMUS, CUCUMBERS, PEPPERS

CHEESE: LOW-MOISTURE CHEESES LIKE CHEDDAR, COLBY, ASIAGO, AND MUENSTER ARE BEST.

MEAT: SALAMI AND PEPPERONI HAVE NITRATES TO INHIBIT BACTERIA.

Avoid using mayonnaise, which is only safe for a few hours, or bring it in individual packets that don't need refrigeration and can be added right before eating.

ECO-PICNICKING TREATS

After cleaning up the park, you certainly don't want to create more garbage. Kabobs (food on skewers) make the perfect picnic food because they don't create any unnecessary waste. No need for plates or utensils. And they are extra sanitary because your fingers don't even touch the food when you use your handy bamboo skewers!

DRINK SODA IN BOTTLES

SANDWICH ON A STICK[1]

These ridiculously easy sandwiches should take you around 15 minutes to prepare and pack in mason jars for transportation.
{Serves 12 skewers}

What You Need

For the sandwich fixings, you only need around 12 of each item (outside of the sliced bread, of course) for each skewer. But you can double the ingredients for larger sandwiches or for double the servings. Remember to bring extra skewers to keep the sandwich-making sanitary, since each time guests go back for more, they will need new skewers.

2 baguettes
24 ounces hard cheese
1 large cucumber
13 ounce family-size hard salami
1 pound cherry tomatoes
1 large jar pitted olives of your choice, whole
1 large jar bread-and-butter pickles
12 to 24 bamboo skewers
Eight 28-ounce mason jars

How to Make It

1. Slice baguettes into ½-inch slices to fill 2 mason jars.

2. Cube the cheese to fill 1 jar.

3. Thickly slice cucumbers to fill 1 jar.

4. Thinly slice salami to fit into 1 jar.

5. Place tomatoes, olives, and pickles separately into their own 3 jars.

6. Place everything in a carrier or cooler.

7. When it's time to eat, remove jar lids, distribute skewers, and pierce your chosen ingredients in any order.

DESSERT ON A STICK

I find it's easier to assemble dessert skewers ahead of time instead of packing up all the ingredients in mason jars for your guests to make. Also, it's easy to double this recipe!

{Makes 6 skewers}

What You Need

    12 strawberries
    12 blueberries
    6 bite-size brownies
    6 marshmallows
    6 bamboo skewers
    Semisweet chocolate chips (optional)
    Small ziplock bag (optional)

How to Make It

1. Prepare strawberries by cutting the leafy ends off.

2. Skewer your ingredients on a kabob stick in this order: blueberry, strawberry, bite-sized brownie, marshmallow, strawberry, blueberry.

3. Optional: Place your skewers on a baking sheet or cooling rack (with a baking sheet or baking mat beneath). Melt semisweet chocolate chips in the microwave and pour the melted chocolate into a small ziplock bag. Cut the tip off one bottom corner of the ziplock bag and drizzle chocolate onto your skewers. Let them dry.

4. Place dessert skewers in a reusable container and pack in an insulated picnic basket or cooler if it's warm out.

17

Pride Month: Fly Your Freak Flag Party

CELEBRATE DIFFERENCES FOR A GOOD CAUSE.

In second grade, my best friend gave me the nickname "Elf" because of my pointy ears. My ears had never really bothered me before, but once she called attention to them, I began to see them differently. I grew self-conscious. When I looked in the mirror, all I saw were my elfish ears, and I hated wearing ponytails because I felt like everyone was staring at them. I thought they made me look like a total freak.

As I grew older, I realized the value of being different, how the things that make us stand out are actually what make us unique and beautiful. So I began to embrace my ears. Today, I can confidently say that I absolutely love my ears. They're actually my favorite facial feature because they're distinct and make me look like, well, me!

We all have things that make us different on the inside and on the outside. Sometimes these differences may make us feel insecure, especially when specific people or society in general tells us they're wrong. There's so much pressure to look a certain way and to be a certain person that it's hard to recognize how cool and important our differences really are.

June is Pride Month, a national celebration of taking pride in who you are. Pride Month recognizes those in the LGBTQ+ community, people who identify as lesbian, gay, bisexual, transgender, queer, or other orientations. The LGBTQ+ community is often discriminated against for being different, but their differences are a natural part of their identity, and

Pride Month is a reminder to take pride in our differences. So in keeping with that theme, throw a Fly Your Freak Flag party!

CALLING ALL MISFITS

What's a freak flag, anyway? According to UrbanDictionary .com, *freak flag* is "a term to describe a person's unconventional thinking, characteristics or physical uniqueness." It's a perfect month to celebrate our differences and, as always, to party!

DRESS LIKE NOBODY'S WATCHING
Because of society's expectations, we don't always wear clothes that truly showcase who we are. Tell guests to come dressed in an outfit that makes them feel authentically themselves. Maybe that means pajamas and messy hair, or maybe that means a pretty dress and lipstick. Everyone feels comfortable in their own way. I love wearing my dad's oversize dress shirts and baggy jeans, even though that's not a typically "feminine" look. This is also a great time to publicly embrace your secret obsession. Do you have a Justin Bieber concert T-shirt that you've always been embarrassed to wear? Put it on!

FREAK JAR: A PARTY GAME
This party game is perfect for a Freak Flag Party of any size.

What You Need
    Index cards or slips of paper
    Pens, pencils, or markers
    Large jar, bucket, or box

How to Make It
1. Have each guest write down something weird, unique, or special about themselves—preferably something that people don't generally know. It can be personal or funny—whatever they're comfortable with! For large parties, have each person write down one fact. For small get-togethers, have each person write down three facts on three different pieces of paper.

2. Next, tell everybody to put their slips in the Freak Jar (or whatever container you choose!).

3. Pick a slip of paper from the jar and read it out loud. Everybody has to guess who wrote it!

HERE ARE SOME FACTS THAT ENDED UP IN THE FREAK JAR AT MY PARTY:

I still sleep in Spider-Man pajamas.

I HAVE NO NAIL ON MY BABY TOE.

When my sister said that my mom was the Tooth Fairy,
I thought that Mom was the actual Tooth Fairy.
For all the children in the world.

I KIND OF BELIEVE IN BIG FOOT.

I can make bubbles come out of my tear ducts
if I blow my nose hard.

I CAN YODEL.

My middle name is really Hildegard.

I CAN BURP THE ALPHABET.

I have a birthmark that looks like the state of Florida.

BIZARRE BITES

Do you love a certain food combination that most people would consider disgusting? I love dipping French fries in milkshakes, for example. A lot of us have strange dishes that we adore. Ask your guests to bring in a batch of their bizarre bites for others to try or serve up one of my favorite suggested combos—that taste *way* better than they look!

FREAKY FOOD COMBOS THAT MIGHT ACTUALLY TASTE GOOD!

Grilled cheese sandwich dipped in strawberry jam
Cream cheese, potato chips, and chives on bread
Peanut butter, pickles, and bacon

French fries dipped in a milkshake
Crushed-up cheese puffs on top of broccoli
M&M's on top of cheese pizza

If your school has a Gay-Straight Alliance club, consider inviting a member to speak about the meaning of Pride Month. Or consider providing information about a local LGBTQ+ resource center to benefit guests who might need somebody to talk to.

Always remember, no matter what anybody says, being a "freak" is cool!

18
Veggie and Dairy Month: Ugly Food Feast

COOK AND SHARE A MEAL USING FOOD WASTE.

We live in a society that often tells us we have to be perfect in order to be accepted. But our society promotes a deeply unrealistic definition of perfection. We're taught to be ashamed if we have a big nose or pimples or pointy ears, which are natural features that make us who we are. Have you noticed how we even have unrealistic definitions of perfection for *all* living things? Have you ever thrown away an apple because there's a spot of brown on its skin or chosen a smooth tomato over a lumpy one at the supermarket? Yup, even plants must look a certain way in order to be accepted. As a result, one-third of the food grown in the world each year is never eaten, and in the United States alone, 40 percent of our food is wasted.

Why is so much good food ending up in landfills when so many people are going hungry? And why are we not talking about this? To start the conversation in my community, I had some friends over for dinner and decided to make a meal from food that would have normally been thrown in the trash. My local supermarket happily handed over weird-looking tomatoes and avocados that they couldn't sell because they were "ugly," and we took home an actual trash bag of juice pulp from their juice bar. We enjoyed veggie burgers made from the juice pulp and garnished with the misshapen vegetables. We also used the brown bananas sitting at the bottom of my fruit bowl to make banana bread.

WASTE NOT, FEED MANY

The first step in solving this issue is raising awareness and learning how to use the food we dismiss as waste. Invite your friends over and throw your own Ugly Food Feast. You may even want to show a food waste documentary. Take it a step further and try to create as little waste as possible with other aspects of the party, like using real plates instead of paper plates, and recycling anything that can be recycled.

Q&A TABLE TOPIC CARDS

Make a deck of eye-opening table topic cards to get your friends talking about the cause while you eat dinner.

What You Need

Index cards (blank ones work best)

Pens

Stickers and other art supplies (optional)

How to Make It

1. Do some research about food waste. Find surprising facts and statistics. Break down these facts into questions and answers to shock your guests. For example:

   Q: How much food waste ends up in landfills?
   A: 97%[2]

2. On the front of your card, print out or handwrite the question. On the back, put the answer.

3. Feel free to decorate your table topic cards with stickers, doodles, glitter, or whatever strikes your fancy.

4. Place the deck in the middle of the table or put a few cards facedown on every plate before your guests arrive. Take turns reading them out loud, and make sure everyone guesses before you reveal the answers.

THE BILL EMERSON GOOD SAMARITAN ACT

Unlike the supermarket in my neighborhood, many stores refuse to donate their ugly food that's headed for the garbage because they believe it poses liability issues. But there's good news! In the United States, stores are protected when they donate their food with good intentions under the Bill Emerson Good Samaritan Act, which allows nonprofit organizations to feed the hungry in their communities. So at my dinner party, I printed out information about local food pantries and copies of the act for my friends to take home, and I challenged them to make sure their supermarkets know that it's safe to donate their food.

FOOD WASTE FACTS!

TABLE TOPIC EXAMPLES

Here are some of my favorite Q&A food-waste shocker stats that I learned from the End Food Waste Now organization, to get you started.[3]

Q: On the top twenty list of greatest landfill contributors, where is food waste listed?

A: *Food waste is the second greatest contributor to landfills.*

Q: How many people don't get enough food for a healthy life?

A: *795 million. One in nine people go hungry.*

Q: How many tons of food do rich countries waste per year?

A: *222 million tons. That's almost as much as the entire net food production of sub-Saharan Africa (which is 230 million tons).*

Q: Is food that is breaking down naturally in landfills harmful to the environment?

A: *Yes, very harmful. Food waste that breaks down in landfills produces methane, a greenhouse gas twenty-one times more powerful than carbon dioxide.*

Q: Which types of food have the highest waste rates?

A: *Fruits and vegetables. Most supermarkets don't accept fruits and vegetables unless they look perfect, forcing growers to throw away tons of perfectly good crops.*

Q: How many times is a piece of food handled before it's touched by the consumer?

A: *At large-format grocery stores, an average of thirty-three times. Shop locally!*

MENU À LA POUBELLE
(MENU OF THE TRASH CAN!)

Follow our suggested menu, or create one of your own. Talk to a supermarket near you about donating their food for your cause, and make sure to visit armed with a copy of the Bill Emerson Good Samaritan Act just in case!

VEGGIE BURGERS
{Makes 4 burgers)

What You Need

- ½ cup bread crumbs or oatmeal
- 2 cups canned black beans, drained
- 1 teaspoon onion powder
- 2 cloves minced garlic
- 1½ cup juice pulp (mostly from vegetables if you can, but some fruit pulp will work too)*
- 1 tablespoon coconut or olive oil
- ¼ teaspoon ground cumin
- ½ teaspoon salt
- 2 teaspoons chili powder
- 2 tablespoons coconut or avocado oil for frying
- 4 hamburger buns
- Toppings and condiments (ketchup, mustard, lettuce, tomatoes, etc.) (optional)

AFTER OUR MEAL, MY FRIENDS AND I WATCHED A DOCUMENTARY ABOUT FOOD WASTE CALLED JUST EAT IT. CONSIDER SHOWING A DOCUMENTARY AT YOUR PARTY TO EXTEND THE CONVERSATION.

How to Make It

1. Throw all ingredients (except the buns and toppings) in a blender. You want the patties to stick together without falling apart or dripping out of your hand, so add more oatmeal or bread crumbs if the mixture is too wet.

2. Form patties. Fry in hot oil until crispy.

3. Place on hamburger buns and add toppings as you see fit.

* See if a local juice bar or supermarket will donate pulp for the occasion. If that's not an option, collect leftover fresh veggie scraps during the week and put them in a blender to create your own pulp.

Supermarkets discard perfectly good produce every morning because it isn't cosmetically pleasing or because it simply didn't sell. If you can rise up early enough to get to the store soon after it opens, you may be able to get some produce for a salad to make this a true no-waste meal.

BANANA BREAD
{Makes 2 loaves. Serves 12 to 16.}

What You Need

Two 8½ x 4½-inch loaf pans
2½ cups all-purpose flour
2½ teaspoons baking soda
½ teaspoon kosher salt
5 to 6 medium overripe bananas
(the browner the better!)
¼ cup vegetable oil
¼ cup olive oil
1 cup granulated sugar
2 large eggs
½ cup sour cream

How to Make It

1. Preheat oven to 350°F. Grease and lightly flour both loaf pans.

2. In a medium bowl, sift together flour with the baking soda, then stir in the salt.

3. Place the bananas in a blender and blend until there are no more lumps. You should have about 2 cups.

4. In a large bowl, whisk together the mashed banana, oil, sugar, eggs, and sour cream until completely smooth. Add the dry ingredients and stir until just combined.

5. Transfer the batter to the prepared pans and bake until dark brown and a toothpick inserted in the center comes out with a few moist crumbs attached (60 to 75 minutes).

6. Place the pan on a wire rack and cool for 15 minutes, then turn the breads out of the pans and allow to cool to room temperature before serving.

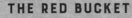

THE RED BUCKET

In my family, we have the Red Bucket. It's been a part of almost every PhilanthroParty we've ever had. We've filled it with everything from water balloons to cans of food, from toys for children to pairs of jeans to be donated. Any time we have a party coming up, we take the red bucket out of the garage and make a sign for whatever it's going to be that day. It's like a faithful companion! Think about what items you have in your home that you can reuse, thus reducing waste and maybe even starting a tradition of your own.

JULY

HERE ARE SOME MORE NATIONAL CELEBRATORY
THEMES FOR THE MONTH OF JULY.

Cell Phone Courtesy Month
Ice Cream Month
Parents' Day—fourth Sunday in July
International Joke Day—July 1
World UFO Day—July 2
Stay Out of the Sun Day—July 3
International Kissing Day—July 6
Chocolate Day—July 7
World Population Day—July 11
Different Colored Eyes Day—July 12
Embrace Your Geekness Day—July 13
Moon Day—July 20
Amelia Earhart Day—July 24

19
National Water Month: Water Walk

LEAD A WALKATHON AND HOST A WATER-THEMED PARTY TO RAISE AWARENESS ABOUT THE GLOBAL WATER CRISIS.

In sixth grade, I learned that 783 million people didn't have access to clean water.[1] I saw videos about girls my age in Africa who had to walk an average of 3.7 miles along dangerous paths in the hot sun to fetch water for their families instead of going to school.[2] The water they carried home was usually dirty and often led to illness. It was so crazy to me that something so basic, something that we take for granted every day, isn't even an option for so many people. And the fact that it's the *girls* who are normally responsible for getting water—and that this task prevents them from going to school—upset me on a very deep level. It hit on so many issues that spoke to my heart: girls' rights, education, and the basic human need for water. I wanted all my friends to know about it, and I wanted to help my community appreciate the basic things we take for granted. Gratitude for what we have is the first step toward helping others who are less fortunate. With this fire lit inside me, my first official PhilanthroParty was born.

Around my birthday, I rallied my classmates and we all walked down a sidewalk on a busy street in town carrying jugs of water, like the girls in Africa (except, of course, we were walking in a safe neighborhood, wearing shoes, and the water we were carrying was purified and safe to drink). Even though our circumstances were way more fortunate, we still got a feel for how difficult this daily chore can be. By personally experiencing (even in this small way) a hardship that is the reality of so many, my friends and I gained a stronger sense of empathy and a much greater awareness. It also helped us *spread* awareness about the water crisis. As we walked, curious people often stopped to ask us what the heck we were doing, which allowed us to explain the water crisis. Afterward, I threw a big birthday party at my house, and instead of birthday presents, I asked for donations to Blood:Water, an organization that helps build wells in regions throughout Africa where clean water is not an option.

WALK A MILE (OR 3.7) IN SOMEONE ELSE'S SHOES

Replicate this historic PhilanthroParty in your own community. In a business district for maximum exposure, or just on your neighborhood street, invite friends to carry jugs of water and put themselves in another's shoes. Ask businesses along your walking route to sponsor you. Afterward, cool down with this water-themed party!

WATER WALK TIPS

1. Before the party, visit the local businesses along your planned route to inquire if they would like to sponsor your Water Walk (bring info on the charity to give to them). On my route, restaurants donated the sales of lemonade for the week, a frozen yogurt shop donated sales from their strawberry-lemonade flavored yogurt, and clothing shops set out donation boxes.

2. Ahead of time, designate a safe route with sidewalks. For kids ages twelve and up, try walking 3.7 miles, the actual length young African girls walk each day. For younger kids, keep the walk under 2 miles long.

3. Ask each guest to bring their own inexpensive gallon jug of water. Suggest purchasing the kind with a handle. Make sure to have extras on hand.

4. Designate adult chaperones to act as crossing guards at intersections.

5. Make signs!

6. Print out cards with information about the water crisis and links to the charity you support. Hand them out to curious bystanders, so they can learn more about the cause.

WATER PARTY GAMES

Because this event celebrates that water is a precious thing, and my home state itself is in a drought, I chose activities that use water in limited quantities.

1. *Water Balloon Piñatas.* Hang six or eight balloons a quarter to half filled with water from tree branches at varying heights. Blindfold the batter and supply a three-foot stick or a baseball bat if you have one. Stand back and form a circle around the player from a safe distance. The player gets six swings to try and break a water balloon. Each one they break is one point. Have a large bucket of extra water-filled balloons on hand to replace the ones that have broken open. Play in a grassy area, so the grass gets watered!

2. *Water Balloons and Spoons Race.* This game is similar to the Egg and Spoon race from the Memorial Day PhilanthroParty (page 71)! Line up holding large spoons and small balloons (size of an orange) filled with water. Set up an obstacle course and race to the finish line while balancing water balloons on spoons. The first one to make it without dropping their balloon wins.

3. *Watercolor Table.* Set up a table with watercolor paints as a relaxing craft. You'll need cups or jars of water, paint brushes, a few sets of watercolor paint, and watercolor paper that you can cut into various shapes and sizes. Don't forget to have some paper towels or reusable cloth rags on hand to clean up any painting mistakes or larger spills.

4. *Spongy Water Bombs Fight* (see below). This is an eco-alternative to a traditional water balloon fight. These sponge "bombs" are reusable, washable, save water, and you'll have no plastic balloons to clean up after your epic water bomb fight. Make as many as you can and reuse them as pool toys and for water fights all summer!

5. *Squirt the Cup* (see next page). Re-create an arcade favorite using simple household items like plastic solo cups and water guns.

SPONGY WATER BOMBS

What You Need

- Bulk bag of colorful new sponges
- Ruler
- Scissors
- String
- Bucket of water

How to Make It

1. Measure 1-inch strips and cut along the long side of the sponge.

2. Gather 6 to 9 strips, mixing up the colors and stacking them in rows of 3.

3. Cut some string to tie them tightly together in the middle.

4. Fan them out to a ball shape and trim excess string.

5. Soak in water and—attack!

SQUIRT THE CUP!
Go head-to-head with your friends in this homemade version of an arcade favorite.

What You Need

2 bull's-eye targets (print out an image)
2 large plastic plates
2 large plastic cups
Two 3-foot wooden garden stakes
Two 15-foot lengths of string
2 high-back chairs
2 water guns
Staple gun
Glue stick

How to Make It

1. Glue a bull's-eye target image to the inside of a plastic plate. Poke a small hole in the center.

2. Poke a small hole in the bottom of a plastic cup, near the edge. Make sure the hole is large enough to let your string move freely through it.

3. Secure the garden stake into the ground.

4. Tie the end of one string near the top of the stake. Thread the other end of the string through the backside of the target and then the bottom of the plastic cup, with the open side of the cup facing away from the target. Pull the string taught and secure it to the back of a chair, which should be about 12–15 feet away from the target.

5. Slide the target to rest against the stake and staple it.

6. Slide the cup to the opposite end of the string, near the chair.

7. Repeat the steps above to make another target station and line it up exactly even with the first one you just built.

8. Instruct players to straddle their chair and, when someone says "Go!," to shoot water into the cup. The player who moves their cup along the string to hit the bull's-eye first wins!

20
National Dance Day: Sock Hop till You Drop

A DANCE PARTY TO COLLECT SHOE DONATIONS.

Think for a minute about the last time you left the house without any shoes on. Maybe running around your neighborhood as a kid? But imagine if that was your reality every day of your life, no matter where you had to walk, what you had to do, or what the weather was like. Imaging if the one pair of shoes you did own was so ragged that you might as well be barefoot anyway.

All over the world, one pair of shoes can make a powerful difference between contracting a disease and staying healthy, the difference between going to school and going without an education, and the difference between having confidence in yourself or being ashamed. Think about all the shoes you've outgrown, and how just one of those pairs could mean the world to one person.

July 26 is National Dance Day. Who wouldn't want to throw a dance party? Add some social good to the fun by telling everyone to take their dancing shoes *off* at the door and put an extra pair in a donation box. Traditional sock hops in the 1950s were school dances with a no-shoe rule to spare the gymnasium floor from scuffs. This shoe-free sock hop is to remind us of those who live in conditions where going barefoot is not a choice.

SOCK IT TO ME!

When you send out your invites for the dance party, remind your guests to wear or bring socks because the dance floor will be a shoe-free zone. Encourage people to wear wacky, brightly colored clothing that allows for maximum movement. Maybe come up with a theme, like space-age sock hop or a classic 1950s sock hop. The issue is serious, but the dance is a chance to go crazy and have fun!

Put together a playlist or use my suggestions, and ask one of your music-loving friends to DJ.

CREATING A PARTY ATMOSPHERE

1. Find a location with plenty of room to dance. Move furniture if needed.

2. Make sure you have great dance music and a sound system that will be loud enough (but not too loud) for the space.

3. Experiment with lighting. Try to find some standing lamps that allow overhead lights to be turned off for a more festive atmosphere. You might also look for some inexpensive LED flashers (more eco-friendly than glow sticks).

4. Finally, for maximum dance-party vibes, see if you can borrow a disco ball from a friend or from your school. And if you come up short, don't worry about spending money to buy one. Make a gorgeous, easy DIY balloon disco ball (see next page). When you shine light on it, it sends sparkly lights dancing around the room just like the real thing!

This is Nicholas Lowinger, another Nickelodeon Halo Honoree. We actually met before the Halo Awards, when we were thirteen years old at a Build-A-Bear Workshop Huggable Hero ceremony. He founded the organization Gotta Have Sole when he was eleven to provide new shoes to kids who can't afford them. You can read about Nick and his incredible work on page 118. Present your guests the option of donating money to buy new shoes through organizations like Gotta Have Sole. For guests who prefer to donate gently used shoes, make sure they are in good condition. They shouldn't have any holes or rips, and they shouldn't be missing any parts, like laces.

Lulu's Nifty Fifties Playlist

In keeping with the sock hop theme, throw it back a few decades and rock around the clock to a few of these oldies but goodies!

Rock Around the Clock
—BILL HALEY

All Shook Up
—ELVIS PRESLEY

My Girl
—THE TEMPTATIONS

Shout
—THE ISLEY BROTHERS

Shake, Rattle and Roll
—BIG JOE TURNER

A Teenager in Love
—DION AND THE BELMONTS

Johnny B. Goode
—CHUCK BERRY

Yakety Yak
—THE COASTERS

La Bamba
—RITCHIE VALENS

DISCO BALL-OONS[3]

Don't have a disco ball? Not a problem! A balloon, some glue, and a bit of glitter works just as well!

What You Need

Glitter or sequins (or both!)
Paper plates
Large balloons
Mod Podge (glue sealer and finish)
Foam craft brush
Ribbon or string
Ceiling hooks or pushpins (optional)

How to Do It

1. Pour glitter or sequins onto a paper plate

2. Blow up as many balloons as you want to glitz up your party.

3. Using a foam craft brush, apply Mod Podge to the rounded half of an inflated balloon.

4. Roll the Mod Podge–covered half of the balloon on the paper plate full of glitter or sequins, making sure that the shiny stuff is evenly applied.

5. Tie ribbon or string to the knot of the balloon.

6. Repeat steps 3 through 5 for each disco ball-oon.

7. Hang them from the ceiling with ceiling hooks or pushpins or tie from a lighting fixture or chandelier.

96

21

Day at the Beach: Seaside Scavenger Hunt

CLEAN UP THE BEACH AND COLLECT TRASH TREASURES TO WIN A SCAVENGER HUNT.

Okay, so by now you know how important water is to me. Not having access to clean water hurts not just the health of so many people but also their chances to make a better life. Water makes up 60 percent of our bodies and 70 percent of our entire world. So I think it's pretty safe to say it's important.

My home state of California is known for its beaches. They border half of our state, and we are a *big* state. But even though we love our ocean views, we don't always take great care of them. Did you know that plastic and debris in our oceans can stay there for hundreds of years? And the more harmful trash is to the ocean, the harder it is for the species within it to thrive. Can you imagine if all our oceans were filled with garbage? Just because they're big doesn't mean it isn't possible. In fact, it's already happening; the Great Pacific Garbage Patch is a massive collection of ocean debris approximately the size of Texas! We can't let this continue. So take action and gather your friends for a beach cleanup and scavenger hunt!

IF YOU DON'T LIVE NEAR THE OCEAN, A RIVER, LAKE, OR CREEK CLEANUP WORKS AS WELL. THE HEALTH OF ALL WATER ECOSYSTEMS IS IMPORTANT!

TRASH FOR TREASURE

Chances are, if you have a body of water in your area, there's likely an organization that protects it. In Los Angeles, I team up with Heal the Bay to host this PhilanthroParty around their scheduled cleanup dates. But you can do it on your own too. After cleaning up, enjoy your day at the beach and raise the fun factor by setting up a beach scavenger hunt competition. As you and your guests pick up trash, have them also follow a scavenger hunt list. Whoever finds the most items on the list wins a prize!

Remember to schedule a time to break, check in with everyone to see how the hunt is going, and eat some ocean-themed snacks.

WHAT TO BRING

Work gloves

Buckets or trash bags

Hand sanitizer

Sunscreen

Bags for scavenger hunt items (attach a list with the scavenger hunt items onto each bag beforehand)

Prize for the winner (see suggestions below)

SCAVENGER HUNT SUGGESTED ITEMS

Here's a list of possible scavenger hunt items to get you thinking. It's unlikely that someone will find all the items, so whoever finds the most wins.

Sea glass (bonus points if it's blue or purple!)

Heart-shaped rock

Rock with a white line wrapped around it

3 purple things

Something you can reuse

Something with the letter Q on it

Money!

The roundest rock you can find

An unbroken shell

A bird feather

A crab shell or claw

Winner's Booty

In the spirit of the party, put together an eco-friendly prize basket for the scavenger hunt champion. Fill a canvas shopping bag with goodies like reusable water bottles and environmentally conscious beach toys (check out Green Toys; they make 100 percent recycled products). You can also fill the bag with DIY eco-crafts like Seed Bombs (see page 52), Bioseed Paper (page 56), Sponge Bombs (page 92), or all-natural Lip Scrub (page 110).

HEALTHY OCEAN SNACKS

Here are some tips for serving yummy, nautical snacks:

1. *Shake an Egg.* Deviled eggs are shaped like the hull of a boat. Add triangle-shaped green, red, and yellow pepper sails.

2. *Octopus Hummus.* Spread hummus on a plate. Cut an orange or yellow pepper in half and slice the other half into strips. Set the big half in the center of the hummus so it looks like an octopus's head. Add eight strips around as tentacles and use sliced olives secured with toothpicks for eyes.

3. *Dolphin Fruit Salad.* Place blueberries in a five-ounce clear plastic cup. Cut a banana in half and split the tip so it forms a dolphin's open mouth. Insert a Goldfish cracker in the slit. Add eyes by poking holes in the skin of the banana with a toothpick. Plant the banana flat-side down in the blueberries so it looks like it's jumping out of the ocean to catch a fish.

CLAM COOKIES

Here's an easy recipe for some sweet seaworthy snacks!
{Makes 12 cookies}

What You Need

- 2½ dozen madeleine cookies
- 12 mini marshmallows
- Pink frosting (add red food coloring to any white ready-made frosting or the Buttercream Frosting recipe on page 164)

How to Make It

1. With a knife, shave the grooved side of 12 madeleines so they lie flat with the smooth side up.

2. Frost the smooth side of 24 madeleines, including the twelve shaved ones.

3. Place a marshmallow in the middle of the frosted side of the original 12 shaved cookies. Place the remaining frosted madeleines on top, grooved side up, to form the shape of an open clam.

4. Pulse the last 6 cookies in the blender until the texture is like sand. Display your clam cookies on top of the crushed cookies for a clambs-on-sand effect.

If your local waterway isn't great for picnicking or swimming, take the party to a local pool or someone's backyard pool to end your day with a splash!

AUGUST

HERE ARE SOME MORE NATIONAL CELEBRATORY
THEMES FOR THE MONTH OF AUGUST.

Family Fun Month

Eye Exam Month

National Water Quality Month

National Smile Week—second week of August

Friendship Week—third week of August

Book Lover's Day—August 9

National S'mores Day—August 10

Relaxation Day—August 15

Senior Citizens' Day—August 21

National Tooth Fairy Day—August 22 (and/or February 28)

Women's Equality Day—August 26

National Dog Day—August 26

Global Forgiveness Day—August 27

22

Lemonade Month: LemonAID War

HOST A LEMONADE STAND COMPETITION TO BENEFIT YOUR FAVORITE CAUSE.

I would have never guessed that a beverage would change my life. But the crazy path I've taken leads back to a pitcher of lemonade. Growing up, I spent summer afternoons at the foot of my driveway, trying to sell lemonade to my neighbors in the sweltering Los Angeles heat. Sometimes a few of my friends and I would set up a stand at a local park. The fun was never in the money but in squeezing the lemons and making the signs and hanging out with my friends. One day, my mom made a simple suggestion on our way to a park: why not donate the money we raise to a charity? From that point on, my friends and I began giving all of our lemonade money to different local charities that spoke to us. I was still having the same great time with my friends, but that handful of change at the end of the day made the experience even better. I felt like I had made a small, positive impact on my community, and for the first time I realized that even though I was just a kid, my actions mattered. That's really when the link between *helping out* and *hanging out* formed for me, and my number one goal with LemonAID Warriors is to help all of you guys recognize that link too!

You've already read about the LemonAID War in the introduction and in the Martin Luther King Jr. Day After-Service Party, but, in short, the boys and girls in my class fiercely competed via lemonade stands to raise the most relief funds for Haiti. Following two weeks of battle, we ended up with $4,000, which was a *total* shock after going home with nickels for most of my lemonade career. So what was the key to our success? Two things contributed: urgency and competition. Urgency, because we wanted to act fast and send aid to ease the ongoing suffering in the aftermath of the earthquake. And competition because beating the boys and demonstrating our mighty feminine strength was essential! That's what gave us the motivation we needed, and that's what

made the LemonAID War our social highlight of the year.

August 20 is National Lemonade Day, and I challenge you to celebrate this supreme beverage by hosting your very own LemonAID War.

LEMONAID STAND STRATEGIES

Coordinate with your friends and create two teams. Determine a starting and ending time and spend the day trying to raise more money than your opponents. At the end of the day, meet at your house to tally the results and have a party to celebrate everyone's success, but especially the winning team's! Prizes are optional because the *biggest* prize in the world is the joy of doing good (of course). These tried-and-true lemonade recipes will attract customers to your stand. And follow my tips to boost your chances of victory!

PICKING A LOCATION

1. You want a high-foot-traffic area to make the most sales with your stand. If you don't live on a street that meets this criteria, check to see if any of your team members live in an area with lots of foot traffic. If anyone's family has a business on a busy road, ask to set up out front. If the high traffic is literally traffic, you'll want a spot where it's easy for people to pull their cars off the road, so they can hop out and buy your lemonade.

2. Parks are tricky. Sometimes you get kicked out. So I always ask the person working at the park's recreation center or give them a call. Also, I never sell lemonade if there is already a snack bar or an ice-cream truck at the park. I don't want to steal their customers and take away from their income.

3. Sports practices or tournaments make great locations, but make sure there's no snack bar. You don't want to take their business either.

4. Check the weather. If it's cold, offer hot chocolate and coffee instead. If it's going to be extra hot or rainy, find a sheltered spot or change the date.

ORGANIZING YOUR STAND

What You Need

A cooler for ice
Several bags of ice, depending on cooler size
Pitchers or Cambro beverage dispensers for holding lemonade
Cup for scooping ice
Cups for serving lemonade
Change fund (Start off with two $10 bills, five $5 bills, ten $1 bills. That's a total of $55.)
Antibacterial gel
Non-latex gloves

1. *Start safe.* Your coolers, thermos, Cambro dispensers, pitchers, and any other item you use to prepare, store, and serve should be sterile. You should have hand-washing options available nearby and antibacterial gel in the stand.

2. *Keep your ice separate in a cooler.* Don't put it in the lemonade because it melts and turns the lemonade watery. Scoop ice into cups, then pour the lemonade on top. Make sure to keep the scoop somewhere other than inside the cooler; the handle shouldn't ever touch ice that's going into people's drinks.

3. *Give everyone a job.* Tasks like taking orders, scooping ice, pouring lemonade, and overseeing the money can be delegated to different people. Don't have people handling money and then handling the drinks. Get your loudest, most confident teammate to make some noise and advertise!

4. *Bring change.* It's called a float: start off with two $10 bills, five $5 bills, ten $1 bills. That's a total of $55. And I know I am repeating these numbers from the What You Need list, but this is important info, my friends! Having a float means that if people want to donate but only have larger bills, you can offer to give them change and avoid an awkward moment!

BOOSTING SALES

1. Ask for donations. I find that I raise more money when I let the customer set the price.

2. For some reason, I've found that colored lemonade sells better, so offer a selection. Pink seems to sell the most. I don't know why.

3. Treats like chips and cookies are huge hits. If you decide to sell snacks, it's a good idea to buy them in bulk.

4. Make sure you have information on the charity you are supporting. It's also smart to keep a list of lemonade ingredients on hand just in case customers ask.

5. Create a sign that your designated advertiser can walk around with to draw attention to your stand.

6. If sales are slow, pass out samples. And be sure people understand the money is going to a good cause.

LEMONAID RECIPES FOR THE TRENCHES

There's nothing like homemade lemonade on a hot summer day! Your customers are bound to love these unique recipes. But before you get concocting, whip up some simple syrup. It's hands-down the best lemonade sweetener ever.

RAISING AWARENESS

If you're like me and passionate about addressing the global water crisis, here's an idea to raise even more awareness at your LemonAID stand. I set up two pitchers of lemonade: one containing normal lemonade, made from lemons, sugar, and pure water, and another filled with Swamp-Ade, which is made with gross, dirty water from a local pond. I ask customers to take their pick. Of course they're going to choose the normal lemonade. Then, I tell them that 783 million people don't have a choice and are forced to drink dirty water every single day. This powerful display puts the water crisis into perspective and lets your customers know that their actions just might save a life. If you decide to set this up at your own lemonade stand, make sure the Swamp-Ade is blocked off, so nobody actually takes a sip—it's just for looks and is poisonous to drink. This is also a great tool to raise awareness at a Water Walk (page 90)!

SIMPLE SYRUP
{Makes about 4 cups, good for 2 gallons of LemonAID}

What You Need

2 cups water

2 cups granulated sugar

Note: You can easily adjust this recipe depending on how much LemonAID you're making. Just remember to use equal parts water and sugar.

How to Make It

1. Stir both ingredients in a small saucepan over medium heat.

2. Bring to a boil, heating until the sugar is completely dissolved.

3. Transfer to a bowl or jar to cool.

BASIC LEMONADE
{Makes 1 gallon (about 16 cups)}

What You Need

2 cups fresh-squeezed or bottled lemon juice (about 10 to 12 lemons' worth)

2 cups simple syrup

Approximately 12 cups cold water

How to Make It

1. Mix lemon juice and simple syrup together in a 1-gallon container.

2. Fill the rest of the container with cold water and place in the refrigerator to chill.

3. Served chilled or over ice.

PEACH-MINT LEMONADE[1]
{Makes about 12 cups}

What You Need
1 cup fresh-squeezed or store-bought lemon juice
(about 4 to 6 lemons' worth)
4 cups peeled and diced peaches (about 6 medium)
2 cups granulated sugar
8 cups water
3 cups packed mint leaves, roughly chopped

How to Make It
1. Combine diced peaches, granulated sugar, and 2 cups water in a medium saucepan over medium heat. Bring to a boil and then let simmer for about 5 minutes, or until sugar dissolves and peaches soften.

2. Remove the saucepan from the heat and add the chopped mint leaves. Let the syrup cool. Once cooled, strain the syrup through a sieve and discard the solids.

3. Mix the remaining 6 cups of water, the peach-mint syrup, and the lemon juice in a container that will hold 12 cups. Place full container in the fridge to chill.

4. Served chilled or over ice.

WATERMELON LEMONADE
{Makes about 12 cups}

What You Need
2 cups fresh-squeezed or store-bought lemon juice
(about 5 to 6 lemons' worth)
6 cups watermelon chunks
2 cups simple syrup
6 cups water

How to Make It
1. Place watermelon chunks and lemon juice in a blender and blend until smooth.

2. In a 1-gallon container, stir in simple syrup and water, and place in the refrigerator to chill.

3. Serve chilled or over ice.

23
National Girlfriends' Day: Beauty Brunch

AUGUST 1

MAKE SPA CRAFTS AND PAMPER YOUR FRIENDS WHILE COLLECTING TOILETRIES FOR OTHERS.

Although it's usually more fun and meaningful to throw a PhilanthroParty around a cause that you personally care about, you might not know what that cause *is* yet. And that's totally okay! Another great launching point is picking an *activity* that you're passionate about. That's a big question I ask people when they want to plan a PhilanthroParty: What do you love? Music? Sports? Rock climbing? (Someone threw a very successful rock-climbing PhilanthroParty once—no joke!)

One of my most amazing, passionate LemonAID Warriors is my friend Madi. Madi supported my earliest LemonAID stands when she was just learning to read and write in first grade, and she has been an active PhilanthroPartier since.

Madi had a lot of answers to the question "What do you like to do?" She loves nail polish and bubble baths and is also an arts-and-crafts enthusiast. We brainstormed and came up with the perfect idea: a Beauty Brunch! One lazy Sunday afternoon when she was nine years old, she invited friends over, and we set up a mini-spa in her back-yard—complete with a craft table for making DIY all-natural lip scrub, a mani-pedi station, and, of course, lots of treats.

In the self-care spirit, guests brought in toiletries to be donated to a local shelter, something they always need. We ended up with well over four hundred toiletries, and Madi and her friends had a wonderfully relaxing day. My high school friends and I also volunteered as the spa "technicians" and loved the party so much that we threw our own!

August 1 is National Girlfriends' Day, so throw your own Beauty Brunch to celebrate your gal pals.

The science behind the ingredients is pretty cool! Coconut oil has vitamins E and K and fatty acids that combat changes in the skin caused by aging. Honey is antibacterial. Raw sugar has glycolic acid to exfoliate and stimulate collagen. Lemons contain vitamin C and citric acid to brighten and exfoliate skin.

PAMPER WITH A PURPOSE

While a spa day is typically a feminine occasion, who says boys can't join in on the fun? No matter what your gender is, we all need to relax once in a while, so I encourage you to go for it. But this time, pamper with a purpose!

Set up three spa stations and have your guests rotate through them. When you send out the invitations, ask them to bring a pair of flip-flops to wear if they plan on getting a pedicure.

PUCKER UP! ALL-NATURAL LEMON LIP SCRUB

This is a great craft because it doubles as a party favor that your guests get to take home. When you set up this station, make sure you have enough of the items below for all of your guests. This recipe makes one individual serving pot of lip scrub, so multiply accordingly.

What You Need

> 1 teaspoon of coconut oil
>
> 1 teaspoon raw honey
>
> 2 tablespoons raw granulated sugar
>
> 1 lemon wedge
>
> Lip balm containers, which can be purchased at a craft store or online
>
> Labels and markers

How to Make It

1. In a small bowl, mix all ingredients and, using the lemon wedge, add a squeeze of lemon juice. The consistency of the lip scrub should be like honey but more granular.

2. Spoon the scrub into small, sterile containers.

3. Create labels: Write what it is, the date it was made, and some directions, like *Use finger or soft toothbrush to scrub on lips.*

ALL ABOUT THAT FACE SPA STATION: ULTIMATE RELAXATION

Time to chill out! Here are a few ideas for the ultimate facials using ingredients that you can probably find in your kitchen. Make sure you provide your guests with headbands or towels to keep their hair back and robes or towels to protect their clothing.

For the eyes:

Cucumber slices

Potato slices

Strawberry slices

Tea bags (Green and black tea bags containing caffeine are the most effective. Just steep the bags in hot water for 3 to 5 minutes, allow them to cool completely, and then squeeze out any excess liquid until they are just damp.)

For the face:[2]

Avocado and Honey Facemask: ½ ripe avocado, 2 tablespoons honey, and ½ teaspoon coconut oil (per person)

Oatmeal Facemask: ⅓ cup instant oatmeal, ½ cup hot water, 1 tablespoon honey, and 1 tablespoon plain, unsweetened yogurt (per person)

Manly Mask (great for guys!): ½ cucumber (peeled, chopped, and pureed in a blender or food processor) and 1 tablespoon full-fat Greek yogurt (per person)

FANCY FINGERS: MANI PLEASE!

Break out your nail files and favorite sparkly polish! Treat your guests to a relaxing mani-pedi. If you can recruit volunteers for the day, this is a great station for them to work.

What You Need

- Tablecloth
- Nail polish
- Nail polish remover
- Cotton balls and Q-tips
- Paper towels or facial tissues (can be rolled and used to separate toes)
- Nail files and small nail clippers
- Alcohol and/or bleach water to sterilize tools if they will be shared
- Bowls of water for hand soaking
- Hand lotion (scented and unscented)

What to Do

How to do a simple at-home manicure:

1. Fill a small bowl with warm water and soak fingertips.

2. Apply nail polish remover using a cotton ball, wiping each nail to remove any old polish or dirt.

3. Clip and file nails to desired length and shape.

4. Moisturize hands with lotion.

5. Wipe remover-soaked cotton ball over nails one last time, to be sure the lotion doesn't prevent nail polish from sticking as well as it could.

6. Paint each nail: Do one line down the center of the nail, then fill it in with a swipe on either side.

CHECK OUT THE PRE-PROM PHILANTHROPARTY CHAPTER FOR NAIL-DESIGN TIPS ON PAGE 65.

24
Back to School:
New Kids on the Block Party

WELCOME NEW KIDS WITH A BACK-TO-SCHOOL GATHERING, AND DONATE SCHOOL SUPPLIES.

It's never easy being the new kid. I changed schools in seventh grade, and I'll never forget how scary my first day was at my new school. Walking onto a new campus for the first time, scrambling to find classrooms, feeling the terror of lunchtime. This school had started in sixth grade, so everybody already had their friend groups, and I had no idea where to sit during lunch. I'll also never forget the one girl who made me feel welcome. She invited me to sit with her and her friends, and it was the greatest feeling. Small acts of kindness go such a long way, and since then I've made it my goal to always reach out to new kids and try to make them feel as welcome as that girl made me feel.

Even though first days of school can be rough, we can feel lucky that we even get to go to school at all. When I went to Uganda during the summer a few years ago, I met a girl named Rebecca. She was fourteen, like me, and we probably would have been entering the same grade. Her dress was old, and she didn't have shoes, and her family was living in a mud hut that most likely lacked access to food and clean water. But rather than asking for any of those things, she asked if my family and I could sponsor her to go to school. It was a life-changing moment for me to realize that school was more important to her than food, water, and clothing. Instead of wanting handouts, Rebecca wanted an education, so she could break the cycle of poverty and take control over her life. That first day of school that I had dreaded was Rebecca's dream.

Access to school supplies is a big obstacle for children trying to get an education—even in the United States. So this back-to-school season host a class party and invite all the new kids to get to know their classmates. Ask guests to pick up some extra school supplies when they're doing back-to-school shopping, and donate them to a global or local organization. I know there's a bunch of great organizations in my Los Angeles community that donate school supplies to those who can't afford them, like my friend Riley's organization Rainbow Pack, for example, which you can read about on page 42.

SO LONG, SUMMER!

This party will make the first days of school a lot easier for the new kids, and the school supply donations will give other students the opportunity to *have* a first day of school. Use some of my icebreakers to get the conversation started. Host your party before school starts or during the first weeks of school.

ICEBREAKER GAMES
Play these icebreaker games to help your guests get to know each other better.

If . . .

Each of your guests writes five to ten questions starting with the word *If* on index cards. Give everyone about five minutes to complete this. Collect the cards and put them upside down in the center. Take turns reading and answering the questions. Here are some sample questions you can have premade to add to the pile.

1. If you could teleport anywhere right now, where would you go?

2. If I gave you $10,000, what would you buy?

3. If you could talk to anyone (alive, dead, real, or fictional), who would it be?

4. If I could grant you one thing to come true this year, what would it be?

5. If you could change one thing about yourself, what would it be?

6. If you could live in any time period in history, when would it be?

7. If you could live one day over, which day would it be?

Draw Yourself

Give everyone paper and pen and five minutes to privately draw a picture conveying who they are without using numbers or words. Collect pictures, mix them up and show them to the group and have them guess who drew it. Each artist then explains how their drawing expresses who they are.

Who Am I? Headbands

Before everyone comes over, write the names of teachers and students on index cards. Have each guest pick an index card out of a hat, making sure that they don't see the name written on it. If you don't have headbands like me, have guests hold up the index cards facing away from them or tape them to their foreheads for extra hilarity. Everybody gets to ask twenty yes-or-no questions to guess who they are (Am I a boy? Do I teach science? Do I play sports?). New kids get to cheat with the yearbook! By the end of the game, the new kids will have learned a lot about their new classmates and teachers.

SCHOOL SUPPLIES FOR DONATION

Before the party, send out this suggested list of supplies that kids can bring to donate. I also recommend contacting the local organization that you will be donating to, to ask what supplies they need.

Pencils
Markers
Crayons
Backpack
Glue
Notebooks
Rulers
Highlighters
Binders

SET UP A CRAFT TABLE TO UPCYCLE EMPTY TIN CANS AND TURN THEM INTO ADORABLE SCHOOL SUPPLIES HOLDERS. ALL YOU NEED ARE SOME CLEAN TIN CANS, BEADS, FABRIC SCRAPS, RIBBON, AND WASHI TAPE. GLUE GUNS ARE OPTIONAL.

Lulu's Favorite Organizations

Even though I encourage you to find your own passion-cause, I recommend that you check out some of my favorite organizations. I'm particularly inspired by the ones founded by kids!

Blood:Water brings clean water and HIV treatment to people throughout Africa. This organization has a wealth of creative campaigns and resources online, and they're great at making personal connections with their young volunteers. My family and I also traveled with them to Uganda to visit the wells my LemonAID Warriors helped fund.

Their World and **A World at School.** Former British Prime Minister Gordon Brown and his wife, former First Lady Sarah Brown, work with the United Nations to ensure that every child gets a safe education without discrimination. I am one of their Global Youth Ambassadors and lead a United Nations Town Hall event for their cause.

DoSomething.org is your ultimate social-action resource. Through their website and their app, they feature creative volunteer campaigns tackling every cause that you can think of. They have mobilized millions of young people around the globe to create change.

NKLA. When I first started working in pet rescue, I didn't realize that every animal in Los Angeles city-run shelters is killed if they aren't adopted. The NKLA initiative, which stands for No-Kill Los Angeles, is working on changing that. They have two excellent adoption facilities and support many local dog rescuers. If you live in a city, see if there are any similar initiatives that you can support!

Room to Read builds libraries and schools in areas without access to education. I helped organize a kid rock concert to help them rebuild schools in Nepal after a terrible earthquake. Although they are a larger national organization, they still sent representatives to my event to speak about their work, which was really cool.

Katie's Krops. My friend Katie Stagliano grew a cabbage in her third-grade science class. Freakishly, it grew to be forty pounds! She donated the cabbage to a local soup kitchen to feed hungry families in her town and was inspired to keep growing food. Now her organization gives grants to kids all over the country to start their own gardens and feed the hungry. You can apply for a grant to grow a garden or donate to Katie's Krops to support her amazing work.

Gotta Have Sole Foundation. When Nicholas Lowinger was young, he realized the value of a good pair of shoes. Besides giving you confidence, well-fitting shoes protect your feet and enable you to go to school. Nick was inspired to start an organization to provide brand-new shoes to homeless children, and he's donated tens of thousands of shoes to shelters in over forty-three states.

Rainbow Pack. Riley Gantt started Rainbow Pack when she was ten years old, after a trip to a local elementary school showed her how many kids couldn't afford basic homework supplies. She now visits underserved schools to deliver backpacks filled with everything a kid needs to finish their homework and succeed.

SEPTEMBER

ADDITIONAL SEPTEMBER EVENTS

HERE ARE SOME MORE NATIONAL CELEBRATORY
THEMES FOR THE MONTH OF SEPTEMBER.

Classical Music Month

International Square Dancing Month

National Courtesy Month

National Grandparents Day—first Sunday after Labor Day

Native American Day—fourth Friday in September

Cheese Pizza Day—September 5

Read a Book Day—September 6

International Literacy Day—September 8

9/11 Remembrance—September 11

Positive Thinking Day—September 13

Citizenship Day—September 17

Constitution Day—September 17

25

Hunger Month: Can Carnival

SET UP CARNIVAL GAMES MADE OUT OF CANNED FOODS AND COLLECT CANNED-FOOD DONATIONS FOR A FOOD BANK.

My earliest exposure to community service was through canned-food drives put on by my elementary school. Rather than hosting a single, weeklong event like most schools, we collected cans every week. Eventually, bringing in canned food became a part of the school's culture. It was something I did without ever really thinking about it too much. It was just a part of my routine. That's how I think service should always be: a part of our routine. Something we just *do*.

In fifth grade, I noticed that some of my classmates stopped paying attention to the canned-food drive as the year progressed. We were the oldest elementary schoolers; many had adopted the super-lame attitude of being "too cool" to contribute to a community cause. Naturally, I decided to throw a party for my class to boost awareness for the can drive and prove that you are *never* to cool to do something good. And so the first Can Carnival was born! I set up carnival games fashioned out of cans in my backyard, such as Tin Tower Toppler, where you race to stack the most cans in two minutes; Can-on Ball Toss, where you knock over a stack of cans with a tennis ball (which is harder than you think); and a tin can-bowling alley with the very pop-punk title Bowling for Soup. Guests won raffle tickets at each station, and we raffled off a cotton candy maker someone had donated. Admission was five or more cans of food, and we ended up with close to five hundred cans. It was such a success that we made it an annual event.

In honor of Hunger Action Month this September, I invite you to host your own Can Carnival. It's a great way to address the needs in your own community and have a super-fun time doing it.

STEP RIGHT UP TO END HUNGER

Set up your Can Carnival in your own backyard or in a local park. Admission is at least five cans of food. I encourage you to first get in touch with your local food bank to see what kinds of food they need the most. When you send out your invites, make sure to broadcast the food pantry's needs so that your canned-food collection will have the greatest impact. With one in five children in America struggling with hunger, healthy food donations are a smart start to address this large problem. Step right up, and let's do our part!

CRAZY CAN CARNIVAL GAMES
Start collecting and setting aside empty, cleaned-out cans from your recycling bin ahead of time. Soda cans and food cans work best. In your invitation, ask guests to bring in a few clean empty cans in addition to the canned foods to donate. (You need empty cans for only a few games—most of these will work with full cans.) Take good care of the cans that people bring in for donation, making sure they are kept clean and that the labels aren't damaged.

1. *Hunger Games.* Stack apples on top of full cans on the steps of a ladder. Knock off the apples with a Nerf bow and arrow. Make sure to compost the apples afterward. Needs: 10 full cans (depending on the size of your ladder)

Because some of these games require empty cans, don't let their contents go to waste! Plan your menu around canned food. Canned fruit is delicious in yogurt parfaits. Use canned beans and tomatoes to make a pot of chili or serve piping-hot canned soup to warm up your guests on this autumn day. The possibilities are endless!

2. *Can-on Ball Toss.* Arrange empty cans in a pyramid. Soda cans work well. Stand back fifteen feet. Knock them over with a tennis ball.
Needs: 28 full or empty cans

3. *Tin Tower Toppler.* See how many cans you can stack on top of each other in one minute.
Needs: 15 empty soda (or soup) cans

4. *Can-Can Competition.* Wear ridiculous costumes and dance the cancan dance in honor of the "can-cans" of foods you are collecting. How many kicks can you do before the music ends? Needs: crazy costumes!

5. *Bowling for Soup.* Line up full or empty cans in bowling pin formation. Knock them down with a basketball.
Needs: 10 full cans

6. *Tin Can Stilts Maze.* Use our instructions to make stilts out of tin cans and walk through a chalk maze in under three minutes. Needs: 2 large empty cans

TIN CAN STILTS

What You Need

Twine or heavy-duty string

2 clean and empty 28-ounce tin cans or empty paint cans

Cardboard tube from a wire hanger

Hammer

Nail

Duct or electrical tape

How to Make It

1. Cut two pieces of string (each around 3 feet long for kids and 4½ feet long for adults)

2. Cut cardboard tube into two 3-inch sections. Thread the tubes onto the twine.

3. Using a hammer and a large nail, make one hole on both sides of each can, near the top of the can.

4. For both cans, thread string through the two holes and trim, so the string reaches mid-thigh.

5. Knot the string securely and hide it within the cardboard-tube handles.

6. Add electrical or duct tape along the bottom edge of each can for slip resistance.

IF THE CANS YOU USE FOR YOUR GAMES ARE IN PERFECT CONDITION AFTER THE CARNIVAL, DONATE THEM! WE COVERED OUR CANS IN PRETTY PAPER TO MAKE SURE THE LABELS STAYED INTACT. HOWEVER, IF THEY ARE THE SLIGHTEST BIT DAMAGED, KEEP THEM FOR YOUR OWN USE. THEY'RE STILL GOOD TO EAT, BUT YOU DON'T WANT TO DONATE DAMAGED CANS.

26
National Teddy Bear Day:
A Caring Campout

SEPTEMBER 9

THROW A CAMPOUT-THEMED SLEEPOVER AND COLLECT STUFFED ANIMALS FOR CHILDREN IN CRISIS.

We all have a favorite teddy bear or blanket. Mine is Bun-Bun. She is a small, simple white (formerly pink) bunny who has miraculously survived my childhood and still lives on my reading chair. I took Bun-Bun everywhere when I was little, and I felt at a loss whenever I left her behind. That's because stuffed creatures are much more important than we realize. They actually serve to help us to feel safer, to create a base that we can take with us to explore the world, or to comfort us in times of need.

September 9 is National Teddy Bear Day. To stick with the bear theme, throw a camping sleepover in your backyard, or even in your living room, and tell guests to bring bears to donate to children in need. Our police station keeps teddy bears and stuffed animals in the station, and some officers carry them in their patrol cars in case they take children into custody or rescue them from dangerous situations. Some kids are afraid of police officers, so keeping a teddy bear handy helps soothe a child during a crisis. Soldiers overseas also carry small stuffed animals to befriend or calm down frightened children in war zones. You know what your stuffed animal meant to you when you were younger. On National Teddy Bear Day, spread a little love in the form of a tender, loving bear!

TEDDY BEAR CAMPOUT

Gather your friends for a cozy night of s'mores, stories, and fuzzy fun! When you send out invites, share these guidelines for making a teddy bear donation. Guests need to bring either new or gently used bears that are free of rips, stains, and any kind of odor. You'll want to pick an organization for the donation and note this in your invite too. Here are some ideas on where to donate:

SAFE: Stuffed Animals for Emergencies
Humane Society
Habitat for Humanity
The Salvation Army

DIY INDOOR SHEET TENT

Important: You're definitely going to need major help from a parent or guardian to build this tent! But the good news is you won't ruin your sheets with this DIY, and the materials cost under $4 per tent.
{Materials make 1 tent}

What You Need

Four 2 x 48-inch pieces of wood molding
One 1¾ x 48-inch poplar dowel
Drill with a ¾-inch spade bit
Tape measure
Twin flat sheet (sheet will not be harmed)
Blankets and pillows for sleeping

These tents are for indoor sleeping or outdoor daytime fun as a cozy play fort in your yard. If you plan on camping outdoors, stick to a traditional camping tent.

How to Make It

1. Drill a hole in the center of each molding, 6 inches from the top.

2. Push one end of the dowel through the holes of two moldings until 1 inch of the dowel has pushed through. It should be snug.

3. Push the other end of the dowel through the holes in the remaining two pieces of molding. Fan out both sets of molding to create an A-frame tent support and adjust to desired height.

4. Drape the sheet evenly over the top dowel. Tie all four corners of the sheets to the four corners of the tent pole at the ground. Use packing tape or heavy-duty string to secure if needed.

5. Create a cozy interior: fill the tent with as many blankets and pillows as you can get your hands on!

PUT TOGETHER CUTE LITTLE COMFORT GIFTS FOR YOUR GUESTS. A WASHCLOTH, TOOTHBRUSH, LIP BALM, AND A MINI TEDDY ARE ALL YOU NEED!

CAMPFIRE FAVORITES

No campout is complete without roasted marshmallows! Whether you're camping in your living room or under the stars, here are some suggestions for making the ultimate indoor or outdoor s'mores.

CLASSIC S'MORES
{Makes 1}

What You Need

1 medium to large marshmallow, roasted

2 graham crackers (each 2½ inches square)

¼ of a chocolate bar (traditionally milk chocolate, but dark chocolate or bars with caramel or other fillings can be a delicious variation)

Note: Make sure to have enough ingredients so that all of your guests can make around 3 s'mores.

**CHANGE IT UP BY
EXPERIMENTING WITH
DIFFERENT FILLINGS
AND COOKIES:**

**PEANUT BUTTER
NUTELLA
OREO COOKIES
CINNAMON GRAHAM
CRACKERS**

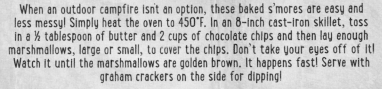

When an outdoor campfire isn't an option, these baked s'mores are easy and less messy! Simply heat the oven to 450°F. In an 8-inch cast-iron skillet, toss in a ½ tablespoon of butter and 2 cups of chocolate chips and then lay enough marshmallows, large or small, to cover the chips. Don't take your eyes off of it! Watch it until the marshmallows are golden brown. It happens fast! Serve with graham crackers on the side for dipping!

27

Labor Day: Party-in-a-Box

FIRST MONDAY IN SEPTEMBER

PLAN AN OUT-OF-THE BOX SURPRISE PARTY FOR UNSUSPECTING PEOPLE WHO MAKE YOUR LIFE BETTER.

On Labor Day, workers are honored with a well-deserved day off. It's not a bad idea to take a moment to think about those who work to make our lives better without being acknowledged for their efforts. When I thought about that, a list of people from my school were the first to come to mind: my bus driver, the crossing guard, and especially the custodians. Teenagers are disgusting, and I totally take for granted that the gross messes we leave behind magically disappear when we return to school the next day. But there's no magic going on. There's a crew of hard-working people I have never met, putting in hours of work while I'm home relaxing.

Throwing parties for people you don't know well but who deserve appreciation can be just as much fun as throwing parties for your friends. Also, if you throw a party for people you don't know, it will be extra surprising because there's no way they'll see it coming! So sometime this month, let Labor Day inspire you by throwing a little surprise party for a person who doesn't know that their work is appreciated. Show them that they matter. Follow this step-by-step plan for the ultimate unconventional surprise party!

PORTA-PARTY!

Let's be real. It would be super hard to sneakily set up an *entire* party on your school bus or in the custodial break room without your surprise party honoree finding out. And sometimes your honorees might not have a schedule that matches up with yours (think of the night shift custodial crew you've probably never even met). So have a mini party with your friends on the weekend and assemble the ultimate Porta-Party. Whether you're there for the surprise or you leave the box for your honorees to find, this portable party is the perfect way to show your appreciation.

PARTY-IN-A-BOX PLAN OF ATTACK
Here are some stealthy tips to help you plan a surprise with maximum impact.

1. *Location.* Scope out your target party zone. See if there's a break room for the custodial staff at your school. Surprise your school bus driver as you and your friends are getting on or off the bus. For the crossing guard or other school staff members, consider leaving the box near their parking space.

2. *Clearance.* If you're setting up your Party-in-a-Box at school, make sure you clear your plan with administration. They probably won't refuse you, but you might need to be supervised. Maybe they'll even want to participate!

3. *Crew.* If you plan on surprising your honoree in person, recruit as many people as possible to give your party ultra impact. However, this is one of the rare parties that you can actually do on your own.

4. *Timing.* If applicable, find out from your school administration what time your honoree starts or finishes work so you know when to set up your box. You may want to go undercover and plan an anonymous party, so set up quickly and then leave. Or you can jump out from behind something and yell, "Surprise!" for the classic surprise-party

effect. If you think there's a chance that an ambush might embarrass or scare the guest of honor, you may want to consider leaving the box for them to enjoy on their own. Remember, celebrating them and giving them your thanks is the goal.

5. *Visuals.* Although your box will be filled with goodies, consider decorating the room for extra flair. Keep it simple. Flowers, balloons, and signs create an instant party atmosphere. Make sure to return to the scene to clean up afterward, of course.

6. *Appreciation.* Make an old-school giant card crammed with signatures and notes from as many people as you can. It's corny and classic and always appreciated. Collect loose change and cash from other students and faculty and buy a gift card for coffee, a manicure, movies, or whatever you can. A girl at my school heard that her bus driver couldn't afford to go to see her family at Christmas. The entire bus chipped in and surprised the woman with a train ticket home for the holidays!

7. *Noise!* If you choose to go the classic surprise party route, blowers, horns, and whistles will make a huge impact. Bring a speaker for your phone and blast some music!

PARTY-IN-A-BOX CHECKLIST

Don't know what to use to assemble your party box? Here are some suggestions.

- Wrapping paper (for decorating the outside of the box)
- A bow (for the top)
- A sign saying *Open me!* or *Surprise!* for the outside of the box
- Giant homemade sign
- Balloons
- Flowers
- Noisemakers

- Party hats
- Giant card
- Little boxes of candy
- Cake, cookies, or other treats
- Pretty, disposable table settings
- Gift card for movie tickets, a manicure, or a favorite lunch spot

OCTOBER

ADDITIONAL OCTOBER EVENTS

HERE ARE SOME MORE NATIONAL CELEBRATORY
THEMES FOR THE MONTH OF OCTOBER.

Breast Cancer Awareness Month

Cookie Month

Domestic Violence Awareness Month

National Diabetes Month

Oktoberfest—dates vary, September and October

Child Health Day—first Monday in October

World Smile Day—first Friday in October

World Egg Day—second Friday in October

Make a Difference Day—fourth Saturday in October

Do Something Nice Day—October 5

World Teachers' Day—October 5

Fire Prevention Week—dates vary, the week of October 9

National Dessert Day—October 14

Dictionary Day—October 16

United Nations Day—October 24

World Pasta Day—October 25

Diwali (festival of lights)—dates vary, often falls in October or November

28

Halloween:
Fang-tastic Costume Party

ON THIS SUGARY HOLIDAY, COLLECT DENTAL HYGIENE PRODUCTS AT YOUR COSTUME PARTY.

For as long as I can remember, Halloween has been my favorite holiday. Part of the fun has always been making my own costumes. When I was three years old, I understood that you were supposed to dress up as something scary. I was terrified of the freeway, so I sported a black shirt with toy cars glued down the back.

While my costumes failed to be scary, the true horror of Halloween is actually its aftermath: the post-trick-or-treat pile of candy that haunts you for months and slowly rots your teeth. For most of us, brushing our teeth is second nature, so we don't always recognize its importance. But oral hygiene affects our overall health, and ignoring it can lead to serious medical problems. This was clearly brought to my attention recently, when I visited an orphanage

in Tijuana, Mexico. It's only three hours from where my family lives, but the poverty in that area is extreme. Before my family left, we asked the orphanage director what they needed most. I expected them to say school supplies or new shoes, but what they desperately needed was dental hygiene products. So before our next visit, my brother, Jasper, emailed local dentists asking for donations, and we ended up with hundreds of brushes and sample-size tubes of toothpaste.

This Halloween, host a costume party, but put a philanthropic twist on it by asking for toothbrushes, floss, toothpaste, or mouthwash as admission. Consider some dental-themed costume ideas. They may not fall into the horror genre, but let's face it: there's nothing scarier than a root canal!

GETTING SPOOKY

Tell your friends that admission to the party is an awesome costume and at least one oral-care product, such as a toothbrush, toothpaste, floss, or mouthwash. Write a form letter asking dentists for oral hygiene donations and attach the letter to your invitation. Encourage your guests to gather even more donations by sending the letter to their own dentists. This is a great way to spread the PhilanthroParty fever by asking your friends to engage with community members and businesses to make the biggest impact. And what dentist would refuse to encourage and spread good oral care in the face of impending Halloween cavities?

DENTAL DISGUISES

Consider these simple costume ideas inspired by the theme. All you need is a T-shirt featuring a giant tooth and a few accessories. I got the tooth image online and used iron-on transfer paper to create these shirts. It's fun to make people guess who you are when you wear these clever costumes.

1. *Tooth Fairy:* Keep it classic with our DIY, no-sew tutu and wings, or give it a "tooth *scary*" spin with vampire fangs and pale makeup. To make an easy DIY wand, cut two identical tooth shapes out of cardboard. Paint them white using acrylic paint and sprinkle on some sliver glitter. Hot glue them to the front and back of a wooden spoon, and ta-da! You have a wand.

2. *Sweet Tooth:* A bouquet of flowers, a giant lollipop, or a big chocolate chip cookie will turn this classic tooth fairy costume into a Sweet Tooth.

3. *Lost Tooth:* Put on a tourist hat, carry around a map, and wear a confused look on your face. You're a lost tooth!

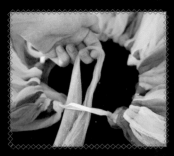

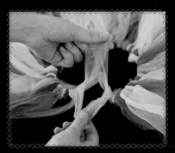

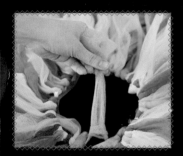

4. *Rotten Tooth:* A prison jumpsuit costume and some handcuffs or a rope is all you need to turn that innocent tooth T-shirt into this Rotten Tooth look. A black-and-white striped jailbird costume or a 1940s gangster costume also work, as long as you can see the tooth peeking out for the gag.

NO-SEW TUTU

Complete any tooth fairy costume with this easy, no-sew tutu!

What You Need

- 75 yards of tulle fabric on a 6-inch spool
- 2 yards of ¾-inch ribbon or elastic (measure to waist)
- Scissors
- Tape

How to Make It

1. Cut about 80 strips of tulle, each 25 inches long.

2. Tie each strip onto the ribbon with a simple slipknot. To do this, you fold your strip in half and tuck the looped end of the folded tulle under the ribbon.

3. Pass the bottom strands of the tulle over the ribbon and into the loop. Pull knot tight so the waist is smooth.

4. Repeat with the rest of the tulle strips. For extra fullness, tie 3 or 4 strips at a time.

GHOULISH GRUB
Here are some ideas to make your food more frightening!

Nightmare Brew: Turn ordinary soda into potion or poison with easy stickers from a craft store or create your own to tape over the existing label.

Graveyard Pudding: Serve your guests some delicious dirt! See Dirt Pudding recipe on page 53; and decorate with gummy worms or other creepy gummy insects.

Doughnut Demon: The snack that bites back! With some false teeth and googly eyes, you can transform doughnuts into little monsters.

Who says the Tooth Fairy is a girl? No one has ever seen the Tooth Fairy, so it's perfectly possible that it's a guy with a ridiculous giant toothbrush wand and a baseball cap. A quick dumpster dive into the recycling bin produced this shoebox and a poster canister. Add some large straws and clear packing tape, and that's all you need for this prop. Jackson with his giant toothbrush went home as the clear winner of this costume contest.

29
Adopt-a-Shelter-Dog Month: Puppy Love Party

HOST A GET-TOGETHER FOR A LOCAL DOG RESCUE.

A couple of years ago, I started a band with a few friends, and we decided to set up a backyard concert. We had another great idea—why not make it a PhilanthroParty?

I had just met a woman with the coolest name ever, Addie Daddio. She hosted a local radio show about animal rescue called *Love That Dog Hollywood!* I was so inspired by her work that I decided to make her charity the philanthropic cause of our concert. We sold snacks and drinks at the concession stand and the proceeds went to *Love That Dog Hollywood!* I also asked Addie to give a quick talk about her work before the concert, so the audience could understand

where the funds were going and learn about animal rescue. Addie went a step further and brought a scraggly, nervous little dog up onstage. She had just rescued him that morning on her way to the concert. His name was Bandit, and he needed a home. After the concert, Addie went home with a $271 donation from the sale of the snacks at our concert. And my family went home with Bandit. We offered to foster Bandit until Addie could find him a permanent home, but I am proud to say that we are foster failures! We couldn't part with him, and now he is a member of our family.

A dog's love is a perfect love. It's hard to believe there are so many dogs out there without anyone to love them back. Around 3.9 million dogs are brought into shelters each year, and only 35 percent are adopted.[1] Show these puppies some love by hosting a get together with your friends, making some homemade dog treats and some DIY dog toys, and then heading over to your local dog shelter for a visit!

LEND A PAW

Contact a local shelter to coordinate a visit for you and your party guests. Ask if the particular shelter you want to visit accepts dog treats, toys, and blanket donations. Every shelter and rescue organization has their own specific needs. If the place you are visiting doesn't accept your donations, with a few phone calls you can easily find another pet rescue that will gladly take them.

For the actual party, ask your guests to bring used towels or blankets. Shelters are always in need of them as bedding and bath supplies for rescued dogs. Spend the afternoon hanging out and making some easy homemade dog treats and doggy toys. Then, pack up your goodies and donations and pile into a car to visit a local shelter! Make sure to coordinate with the shelter on a time to visit to ensure that your guests will get to spend time with the pups.

TREATS FOR DOGS (AND THEIR HUMANS!)

Everyone deserves a treat sometimes. This first treat recipe is for dogs *only*. Check out my Puppy Chow recipe on page 138 for some human-friendly food.

HOMEMADE TREATS (FOR DOGS)[2]
{Makes about 5 dozen}

What You Need

- 1 cup all-purpose flour
- ¼ cup wheat germ
- ¼ cup brewer's yeast
- 1½ tablespoons canola oil
- ½ cup chicken stock

How to Make It

1. Preheat oven to 400°F.

2. Mix dry ingredients in one large bowl and wet ingredients in another.

3. Add wet to dry and mix it all together until it clumps into a ball of dough.

4. On a lightly floured smooth countertop or large cutting board, roll out the dough using a rolling pin (or even an old bottle—washed and dried, of course).

5. Use cookie cutters to cut out the treats or shape them however you like.

6. Place on a baking sheet and bake for 20 minutes.

PUPPY CHOW MIX (ONLY FOR HUMANS)
{Makes approximately 9 cups}

What You Need

- 1 cup semisweet chocolate chips
- ½ cup peanut butter
- 9 cups crispy rice cereal squares
- 1½ cups powdered sugar

How to Make It

1. In a saucepan on low heat, melt the chocolate. Add peanut butter and mix until smooth. Remove from heat.

2. Pour melted chocolate and peanut butter into a large bowl, add cereal, and stir gently until coated. Let it cool.

3. Pour powdered sugar into a large plastic bag, add cereal mixture, and shake until it is well coated in sugar. Store in an airtight container. Keeps up to a week.

DOG TOY DIY

Here's a great upcycle DIY to make with your guests. All you need to do is collect empty plastic drinking bottles and old T-shirts or socks that are too worn to donate. Dogs love the crinkling sound the plastic bottle makes when they chew on the toy. And the loose ends are great for tug-of-war!

What You Need

Empty 16-ounce water bottle (no cap)
Old calf-high athletic sock or old T-shirt
Sewing machine or needle and thread (optional)

How to Make It

1. For the no-sew version, simply put your empty water bottle into the sock and tightly tie the open end of the sock in a knot.

2. If you are using a T-shirt, cut an 8 x 14-inch rectangle of fabric from the torso. Fold it in half to form a 4 x 14-inch rectangle.

3. Sew up the top 4-inch side and sew the open 14-inch length of the fabric, leaving the bottom open.

4. Slide the empty water bottle into the sleeve and sew up the end right at the bottom of the bottle, leaving a 6-inch flap below.

5. Optional: Cut flap to create ½-inch fringe.

30

International Day of the Girl: Calling All Feminists Party

CREATE A CONVERSATION ABOUT WOMEN'S RIGHTS THROUGH DISCUSSION AND A MOVIE SCREENING.

I'm proud to call myself a feminist! A feminist is anyone, male or female, who advocates for and supports the rights and equality of women.

The first time I remember feeling really strongly about global gender inequality was when I heard about the water crisis in Africa and learned that girls my age were the ones required to miss school and walk treacherous roads, carrying heavy jugs to fetch water for their families. The idea of a girl my age being deprived of both education and water is just unbearable to me. I love school. I'm one of those people who even loves doing her homework! I appreciate

my education and feel grateful that I have access to it, especially now that I realize so many kids don't.

International Day of the Girl is a day designated by the United Nations "to help galvanize worldwide enthusiasm for goals to better girls' lives, providing an opportunity for them to show leadership and reach their full potential."[3] Day of the Girl focuses on such issues as negative media images and messages, teen relationship abuse, child marriage, and of course, girls' access to education. Throwing a celebration on this day can be as big as a benefit concert or as small as this simple PhilanthroParty. I invited a small group of guys and girls to play football and to enjoy a feminist favorites feast.

Then we watched a documentary called *Miss Representation* and invited a guest to lead the discussion after. We all were inspired to keep advocating for equality in our daily lives and on a global level. It's amazing how much good can come out of one simple night.

GIRLS JUST WANNA HAVE FUNDAMENTAL RIGHTS!

Once you decide the type of party you are going to throw, make sure you also plan something that will keep guests informed about the purpose of your party. Either invite someone in to speak about women's rights or set up an information booth about the many areas the UN is trying to raise awareness for with this special day. And in order to foster a productive conversation about equal rights, make sure to include boys!

KIERA IS A SUPERSTAR VOLUNTEER FOR LEMONAID WARRIORS AND AN ALL-STAR ATHLETE. SHE LOVES PLAYING FLAG FOOTBALL WITH THE BOYS AT RECESS BECAUSE THERE ARE NO GIRLS' TEAMS AT HER SCHOOL. THERE WAS ALSO A STRICT BOYS-ONLY LEAGUE POLICY THAT APPLIED TO ALL SCHOOL FLAG FOOTBALL TEAMS. KIERA, WITH THE FULL SUPPORT OF HER TEAMMATES, DECIDED TO CHANGE THINGS. THEY SUCCESSFULLY PETITIONED THE LEAGUE TO ALLOW GIRLS TO PLAY FLAG FOOTBALL, AND KIERA MADE HISTORY AS THE FIRST FEMALE FLAG FOOTBALL PLAYER.

FEMINIST FAVORITES FEAST

Ask guests to bring a dish associated with their favorite woman in history. Did you know Emma Watson loves vegetarian stuffed peppers? That Oprah loves a turkey-and-cheese panini she calls a Love Sandwich? And that Susan B. Anthony adored a good old-fashioned sponge cake? Do some internet research and get creative.

EMMA WATSON'S STUFFED PEPPERS

Emma Watson made a brilliant speech at the United Nations to launch the #HeForShe campaign, which engages men and women to dismantle gender inequality. I was so impressed that I became immediately drawn to all things Emma! I even wrote down her favorite recipe when she talked about it on a talk show. I experimented with it, tweaked it a little, and filled in the blanks. Enjoy!

What You Need
{Serves 6}

- 3 medium red or yellow bell peppers
- 1 onion, diced
- 12 cherry tomatoes, halved
- 4 tablespoons pesto
- Shallots
- Cashews (optional)
- 1 clove garlic, minced
- 1½ teaspoons olive or avocado oil
- Honey drizzle

How to Make It

For an easy raw version: Cut peppers in half. Scoop out seeds and white matter. Place cut side up on baking sheet. Combine remaining ingredients (except honey and oil) in a bowl. Stuff the peppers with mixture. Drizzle with honey.

For a roasted version: Preheat oven to 400°F. Place the halved and seeded peppers cut side up on baking sheet and drizzle with ½ teaspoon oil. Roast for 25 minutes or until tender. Remove and cool a bit while you make the stuffing mixture.

Combine remaining ingredients (except honey and oil) in a bowl. In a medium pan, heat 1 teaspoon of oil over medium heat. Sauté the stuffing for 5 minutes. Remove from heat and spoon the cooked stuffing into the roasted pepper halves. Return to the oven for 10 minutes. Drizzle with honey and serve hot.

Lulu's Favorite Girl Power Movies

He Named Me Malala

Girl Rising

Miss Representation

Half the Sky: Turning Oppression into Opportunity for Women Worldwide

It's a Girl!

The Punk Singer

Girls Rock

GET A SPEAKER

Invite a woman in your community who has done something impactful to share her story with the group. (We invited a woman who was running for mayor in Los Angeles, and to our surprise, she came!) Or screen a movie from my list of female-empowering flicks. During the movie, have guests fill out index cards of questions they'd like to discuss. Ask each guest to bring a guest—a woman who has had an impact on their life. Invite each guest to share their experiences with the group and engage in a discussion afterward.

GIRL POWER PLAYLIST

Make a playlist filled with upbeat, empowering songs. Here's my ultimate Girl Power Playlist!

"Hot Topic" (Le Tigre)

"Respect" (Aretha Franklin)

"Looking for a Fight" (Bleached)

"I Love It" (Icona Pop)

"Run the World (Girls)" (Beyoncé)

"Just a Girl" (No Doubt)

"Rebel Girl" (Bikini Kill)

"Jane" (Girlpool)

"Independent Woman" (Destiny's Child)

"Wannabe" (Spice Girls)

Causes Lulu Cares About

BY TOPIC

Water

There is nothing more basic than our need for clean water. I was eleven years old when I learned that over 700 million people don't have access to clean water. I created water-related community events to raise money and awareness for this cause. My Water Walks (page 90), LemonAID Stands (page 102), and Backyard Concert Series (with guests ranging from young local musicians to bands like Hanson) have given clean water to more than four thousand people.

Food

Like water, food is a human necessity. One of my favorite PhilanthroParties is the Can Carnival (page 120), when my LemonAID Warriors and I set up carnival games out of cans. Through these crazy carnivals, we've collected almost 2,000 cans for our local food bank. Also, we have a community garden that is sponsored by teen activist Katie Stagliano of Katie's Krops. She gives grants to kids who grow food to feed the hungry in their community. My brother, Jasper, runs our garden in our backyard, and local Warriors volunteer to help him. From the harvest, they later host dinners at shelters.

Education

While it might not be as obvious as food or water, education is a human right. Education gives us control over our futures and power over our lives. It's so important that we fight for every child's right to a safe education without discrimination. Host your own Follow the Reader book club (page 37) or Back to School: New Kids on the Block Party (page 113) to support this very worthy cause.

Gender Equality

Gender inequality is an issue that plagues the entire world. While women have made some massive progressions in the United States, we still have a long way to go. From ending the wage gap to creating a culture that respects women equally, it's important to take action and stand up for women's rights—regardless of your gender. We also can't forget about the bigger picture. Many girls around the world are prevented from going to school, are forced to marry at a young age, and are more vulnerable to violence, among other issues. Stand up for women's rights by throwing your own Calling All Feminists Party (page 140).

BY ORGANIZATION

Here are some reputable, established organizations. Although I encourage you to check out my favorite causes, it's important to explore a cause that speaks to *you*.

United States Fund for UNICEF fights for the rights and well-being of the world's most vulnerable children. UNICEFUSA.ORG

DirectRelief. When disaster or tragedy strike, this organization responds with medical and rescue aid to places in the United States and around the world. DIRECTRELIEF.ORG

Malala Fund. Founded by Malala Yousafzai, the Malala Fund aims to enable girls to complete twelve years of safe, quality education so that they can have power over their lives and be positive change-makers in their communities. **MALALA.ORG**

The Conservation Fund protects over 7 million acres of land in the United States and the wildlife who call this land their home. **CONSERVATIONFUND.ORG**

Point Foundation offers scholarships and support to LGBTQ+ students. Nearly one-third of LGBTQ+ students drop out of high school due to harassment, violence, and isolation—nearly three times the national average. **POINTFOUNDATION.ORG**

NOVEMBER

ADDITIONAL NOVEMBER EVENTS

HERE ARE SOME MORE NATIONAL CELEBRATORY
THEMES FOR THE MONTH OF NOVEMBER.

Child Safety and Protection Month
National Adoption Awareness Month
National Novel Writing Month
Native American Heritage Month
Daylight Saving (time change)—first Sunday in November
Young Readers Day—second Tuesday in November
Sandwich Day—November 3
Book Lovers Day—November 5
Marooned without a Compass Day—November 6
Veterans' Day—November 11
Sadie Hawkins Day—November 13
World Kindness Day—November 13
Clean Out Your Refrigerator Day—November 15
America Recycles Day—November 15
National Philanthropy Day—November 15
Take a Hike Day—November 17
World Peace Day—November 17

31
Sweater Weather: Heartwarming Party

HOST A WARM AND COZY GATHERING AND DONATE SWEATERS TO THE HOMELESS.

I'm going to be totally honest: My first year of high school, I was really nervous to throw a PhilanthroParty, which was so silly because my PhilanthroParties in middle school were always a huge hit with my friends. But parties in high school are known for being crazy and out of control, and I didn't know if an older, cooler teenage crowd would take the social-good element seriously. Turns out I was completely wrong! One November, I made a presentation to my high school about LemonAID Warriors, and the minute it was over, two of my friends eagerly approached me with a brilliant idea.

Hands-down, the best part about fall and winter in Los Angeles is that after many long months of jean shorts and tank tops, we *finally* get to wear sweaters. So my friends wanted to throw a Heartwarming Party to celebrate the occasion. Everyone wore their favorite sweater and brought in an extra sweater or two to donate to a local shelter. We had an amazing time playing board games, drinking hot chocolate, and just hanging out. At the end of the day, we had collected a *heap* of sweaters that made the holiday season a lot warmer and cozier for people who would normally have been left in the cold. But social good wasn't the theme of the night. Although everyone at the party was doing something to help others, it wasn't a charity event—it was a party. All it takes to turn a regular party into an awesome PhilanthroParty is simply adding a small action for a cause.

Although this party was thrown and attended by teenagers, the sweater party is totally versatile. You can easily turn any holiday (or preholiday) gathering into a sweater-themed party, so I encourage you to spread the warmth this holiday season and dream up a PhilanthroParty of your own!

SWEATER-WEATHER CHEER

I guarantee that you, your family, and your friends have gently used sweaters that rarely get worn and are just sitting, neglected, in closets. Here's a twist I have added. When going through my family's closets in search of sweaters to donate, I found some hilariously ugly fashion disasters. Since everyone at the party will be rummaging for donations like me, they will likely find some ugly treasures too. Invite guests to wear their sorry sweaters and host an Ugly Sweater Contest! Make paper prize ribbons for the winners. Then, if the sweater is in good condition and if you can part with it, donate it at the end of the party.

SWEATER MAKEOVER

Here's an easy way to transform an old sweater into party-ready attire by using materials you probably have lying around at home.[1]

What You Need

- Ruler
- Plaid flannel or other fabric
- Iron-on adhesive paper
- Fabric scissors
- Iron and ironing board
- Stencil
- Paper scissors
- Pen or marker
- Sweater

How to Make It

1. Measure an 8 x 9-inch piece of an old plaid flannel and an 8 x 9-inch piece of adhesive paper. Cut them out using fabric scissors.

Here are some ideas to add an ugly twist to any sweater!

Sew on mini ornaments

Sew or use fabric glue to attach LED battery Christmas lights

Hot-glue small bells

Hot-glue craft pom-poms everywhere

Hot-glue a tinsel garland around your sweater to make yourself look like a human Christmas tree!

2. Set the iron to medium heat with no steam. Place the iron-on adhesive paper on the wrong side of the flannel, with the shiny side down. Press on the paper until it adheres to the fabric. This should only take a few seconds.

3. Print out a stencil of your choice from online or draw one by hand. It should be a silhouette, and make sure it's under 8 x 9 inches. Keep it classic, a heart or a star, or an animal, like a cat or a bunny rabbit. A reindeer's head, Christmas tree, or menorah are perfect for the upcoming holiday season.

4. Cut out your stencil using paper scissors. Then, trace it onto the back of the iron-on adhesive paper that's adhered to the fabric. Use fabric scissors to cut along your outline.

5. Lay your sweater flat on an ironing board. Peel off the adhesive paper and place the fabric, adhesive side down, in the center of the sweater. Iron it on.

AWARD RIBBONS FOR UGLY SWEATER CONTEST

Follow these steps to create adorable DIY award ribbons for the winner of your Ugly Sweater Contest! Make these ahead of time or get your guests involved and set up a craft table so they can help make them.

What You Need

Two 2 x 12-inch strips cut from patterned cardstock

Hot-glue gun and glue

Ribbon

2½-inch diameter circle cut from plain cardstock

2 x 2-inch square cut from cardstock (for back; you won't see this)

Safety pin or button-backs from the craft store

Decorating material (rubber stamps, markers, stickers)

Note: This makes 1 giant prize ribbon. You can make a smaller ribbon by using 1-inch-wide strips.

How To Make It

1. Fold the strips every half-inch back and forth like an accordion. Glue them together to make one long zigzag strip. Then glue the ends of the long strip to make a circle.

2. Set it upright, gather the top edge of the circle toward the center, and then gently flatten it into a circle, or rosette.

3. Use hot-glue gun to glue square cardstock to the center of the rosette's back. This will help flatten the rosette and keep it in place.

4. Decorate your circular cardstock piece. It's the center of your prize ribbon. You can use rubber stamps, markers, or stickers, or go freehand to write *First Prize* or *Ugliest Sweater* or *Winner* on big ribbons. Glue it to the center.

5. Hot-glue the safety pin or button-back to the square cardstock on back, making sure it is positioned so the writing on the front center piece hangs straight.

6. Hot-glue the ribbon below the safety pin and trim it to your liking.

CHOCOLATE TO WARM THE SOUL

Nothing is better than a mug of hot chocolate on a chilly day. Here are some different takes on classic hot cocoa.

YOUR BASIC HOT CHOCOLATE
{Makes 1 mug}

What You Need

1 to 1½ ounces dark chocolate, roughly chopped (about ¼ cup)
1 cup milk

How to Make It

1. In a double boiler over medium heat (or a heatproof bowl set over a small saucepan filled with 1 inch of water), melt the chocolate until smooth. Remove from heat.

2. In a small saucepan, heat the milk over medium-low heat and slowly add in the melted chocolate, whisking continuously.

MEXICAN HOT CHOCOLATE
{Makes 1 mug}

What You Need
- 1 to 1½ ounces dark chocolate, roughly chopped (about ¼ cup)
- 1 cup milk
- ½ teaspoon ground cinnamon
- ¼ teaspoon ground cayenne pepper
- Cinnamon sticks
- Whipped cream

How to Make It
Follow the basic hot chocolate recipe steps. Add the cinnamon and cayenne pepper and whisk to combine. Garnish with a cinnamon stick and whipped cream.

THESE CHOCOLATE-DIPPED STIRRING SPOONS ROLLED IN CRUSHED PEPPERMINT CANDY ADD AN EXTRA CHOCOLATEY RICHNESS TO YOUR HOT COCOA.

PEPPERMINT WHITE HOT CHOCOLATE
{Makes 1 mug}

What You Need
- 1 to 1½ ounces white chocolate, roughly chopped (about ¼ cup)
- 1 cup milk
- ½ teaspoon peppermint extract
- Candy canes
- Whipped cream

How to Make It
Follow the basic hot chocolate recipe steps. Add the peppermint extract and whisk to combine. Garnish with a candy cane on the side or crush the candy into small pieces, add whipped cream to the hot cocoa, and sprinkle the crushed candy on top.

32

Thanksgiving: Leftovers Potluck Feast

FOURTH THURSDAY IN NOVEMBER

INVITE GUESTS TO BRING CREATIVE DISHES USING THEIR THANKSGIVING LEFTOVERS AND TO DONATE CANNED GOODS TO A FOOD BANK.

The big Thanksgiving feast is the real star of this holiday season. But for me, the moment I finish my pumpkin pie, I start looking forward to the leftovers. Every year, on the day after Thanksgiving, my family hosts a Thanksgiving Leftovers Potluck Feast. Each family brings in a dish using as many leftover ingredients as possible. Recently, we've started asking people to bring ten canned goods each, and we call our local food bank ahead of time to see what they need most. During the holidays, food banks often have  a huge influx of holiday food but not enough staples. They end up with shelves full of pumpkin and cranberry sauce and not enough protein-filled foods like peanut butter and tuna. That's why it's important to remember to coordinate with the cause or charity that you are hoping to help when you start your party planning. It's all about giving wisely to make the biggest difference.

For your own potluck, make sure that when you invite your guests you include the list of suggested foods the food bank needs. Encourage non-holiday food staples so that your donations have the biggest impact. I put a twist on our family leftovers-party tradition by adding a DIY recipe book activity. Our guests get creative and kind of competitive about their tasty transformations. Everyone ends up scrambling to swap recipes and share their kitchen secrets. With this DIY, each guest can leave with a useful little recipe book full of do-over dishes!

THANKSGIVING FEAST ROUND 2

Hosting a Leftovers Party is super easy since everyone is bringing something to share. You may want to coordinate with guests to make sure you get a variety of dishes. You don't want to end up with four turkey casseroles! Some online invitation sites have a potluck sign-up option to help guests track the menu and choose dishes according to what you need. Punchbowl .com and SignUpGenius.com are two I use. And I usually provide a simple green salad because that's the dish no one wants to bring, and yet fresh greens are key to balancing out the heavy food!

FOOD FOR THOUGHT

Don't let all that delicious leftover holiday food go to waste! Use it up in these delicious dishes. Ask guests to send you their recipes the day before the party, so you can print them out on index cards. Then place printed recipe cards in front of their corresponding dishes and empty recipe books at the end of the buffet for your guests to fill. I decorate the covers of inexpensive 4 x 6 plastic photo albums for my guests to fill with recipe cards.

LEFTOVERS CASSEROLE
{Serves 10 as a side dish}

What You Need
Cooking oil spray
2 cups stuffing

154

2 cups chopped turkey meat

½ cup cranberry sauce

2 cups mashed potatoes

1 cups cooked vegetables (beans, corn, carrots)

1 cup turkey gravy

¼ cup milk

¼ cup chicken broth

Use leftover pie dough to cover the casserole or
top with ½ cup French fried onions. (optional)

How to Make It

1. Preheat the oven to 400°F.

2. Grease an 8 x 18 glass baking dish with cooking oil spray.

3. Layer ingredients in this order: Stuffing, turkey, cranberry, mashed potatoes, cooked vegetables, gravy mixed with milk. Drizzle chicken broth over the top of the assembled casserole.

4. Cover with foil and bake for 40 minutes. Optional: If you choose to cover with extra pie dough, make a few small slits in the crust to vent steam and bake the casserole uncovered on the bottom rack. Or uncover and sprinkle with ½ cup French fried onions during the last 5 minutes of cooking.

THANKSGIVING LEFTOVERS GRILLED CHEESE
{Makes 1 sandwich}

What You Need

Cooking oil spray

2 slices sourdough bread (any bread will work)

4 slices provolone or sharp cheddar cheese, or
about ½ cup brie or other soft cheese

¼ cup cranberry sauce

2 slices turkey

¼ cup stuffing

4 tablespoons mayonnaise

How to Make It

1. Heat a large skillet over medium heat. Lightly spray with cooking oil.

2. Spread mayonnaise on both sides of the slices of sourdough bread and place them in the skillet.

3. Place one slice of cheese on each open face of the bread. Let the cheese melt for 4 to 5 minutes.

4. Add the stuffing, turkey, and cranberry sauce on one side of the bread and place the rest of the cheese over it. Cover pan to quickly melt the cheese.

5. When the cheese is melted, put the other piece of bread onto the filled side and flip with a large spatula. When both sides of the sandwich are golden brown and all the cheese is melted, remove from heat. Serve warm.

LEFTOVERS RECIPE BOOK

Have guests collect recipes for each dish and assemble their own cute Leftovers Recipe Books to take home.

What You Need

    Guests' recipes (before the party)
    Index cards
    Paper cutter or scissors
    Dollar store 4 x 6-inch plastic photo albums (one per family)
    Washi tape (optional)

How to Make It

1. In your invitations, ask guests to email you their leftovers recipes.

2. Format all recipes for 4 x 6-inch index cards.

3. Print out enough copies for each guest. Trim to size.

4. Create a 4 x 6-inch cover for your Leftovers Recipe Book. Optional: You can also set up a craft table at your party and invite each guest to make their own cover on a 4 x 6-inch index card.

5. Slide the cover card into the clear plastic page at the front of the photo album.

6. Optional: Decorate binding with washi tape.

7. When you set up your buffet table, place recipe cards in front of their corresponding dishes. At the end of the buffet line, stack empty recipe books for guests to insert the recipes they collected.

33
National Games Day:
Game Night Tournament

NOVEMBER (DATE VARIES)

FOSTER A HEALTHY COMPETITION AND LET THE WINNING TEAM CHOOSE WHERE TO DONATE THE POT.

By now you probably know three things about me:

1. I love to make change in the world, no matter how big or how small.

2. I love a little friendly competition. It ups the stakes and makes people work harder. (Except when there are balls or pucks involved. My unhealthy fear of getting hit in the face with fast-approaching round things has ruined sports for me forever.)

3. I love my friends and family, and spending time with them is a top priority for me.

Given those three things, it's not surprising that I love board games, especially when used for a charitable purpose!

Invite your friends over for a game night and have them throw $5 each into the pot. Divide into teams and start playing. At the end of the night, the team who has won the most games gets to donate the entire admission bucket to a charity of their choice.

SCORE BOARD

TEAMS	TWISTER • CHARADES • TRIVIA • CLUE •	TOTAL
RED TEAM		
BLUE		

Because the winning team will choose a charity, make sure they choose wisely! Point them to Charity Navigator (CharityNavigator.net) and see page 178 for tips on vetting charities. In your invitation, you may want to share a list of causes and organizations that you've already vetted, so your guests have a chance to check them out before the fun begins.

GAME NIGHT DECORATION IDEAS

1. String playing cards from ribbon and use as pennant garland or hang from the ceiling. Use a hole punch to make 2 holes about ¾ inch apart and centered near the top of each playing card. Lace the ribbon through the holes and repeat with as many playing cards as you like for the length you want.

2. Use a Twister mat as a tablecloth. (Wipe it down well with disinfectant first.)

List of Lulu's Favorite Board Games

Here is a list of some of my favorite games. You'll have a blast playing these during your Game Night Tournament.

**SCATTERGORIES
APPLES TO APPLES
CATCH PHRASE!
CANDY LAND
TABOO
PICTIONARY
UNO
RUMMIKUB**

3. Use Scrabble stands and tiles to spell guests' names for place settings. Or use Scrabble tiles to decorate cupcakes (but wash them first). I found these cute wooden Scrabble tile mock-ups in the scrapbook section of a craft store, and they made perfect cupcake toppers!

4. Customize your water bottles. Download fake board game money and tape around the bottle.

A NOTE ABOUT SCORING

It's important to devise a scoring system ahead of time. While team board games work best, like Catch Phrase and Taboo, many board games are for single players, such as Candy Land and Scattergories. So when playing single-player board games, award the winner three points for their team, second place earns two points, and so on.

DICE COOKIES
Use our easy no-chill Sugar Cookie recipe on page 21 to create adorable dice cookies. I used a square plastic container lid as a cookie cutter, white premade frosting, and brown M&M's.

PLAYING CARD CAKE STAND

What You Need

Large round cookie tin, like people give
   during the holidays
Hot-glue gun with glue
½-inch ribbon
Deck of cards
Scissors

How to Make It

1. Turn tin upside down.

2. Cut ribbon the length of the tin's circumference.

3. Hot-glue the playing cards to the rim of the cookie tin,
   side by side but slightly overlapping. Alternate red and
   black cards.

4. Glue the ribbon to the top of the cards along the rim of
   the tin to give it a finished look. Use to serve treats for
   your guests.

DECEMBER

HERE ARE SOME MORE NATIONAL CELEBRATORY
THEMES FOR THE MONTH OF DECEMBER.

Write to a Friend Month

Bathtub Party Day—December 5

Human Rights Day—December 10

Ice Cream Day—December 13

Solstice—date varies, but usually around December 21

Boxing Day—December 26

New Year's Eve—December 31

34

National Cupcake Day: Traveling Bake Sale

DECEMBER 15

TAKE CUPCAKE PREORDERS AND SCHEDULE NEIGHBORHOOD DELIVERY. DONATE PROCEEDS TO TOY DRIVES.

Really, I'm more of a pie girl. But I completely understand the cupcake's appeal, especially considering its portable, self-contained design. No plates or utensils needed. There's nothing to slice. They don't need sauces or creams. It's a tidy little marvel of efficiency!

National Cupcake Day is December 15, which definitely calls for a bake sale PhilanthroParty. However, since it is December, it's probably too chilly outside to set up an effective outdoor bake sale. So bring the bake sale to your customers! Organize a slightly unconventional but equally fun Traveling Bake Sale with your friends. With your earnings, you can all go shopping for toys to fill those toy-drive donation boxes that are everywhere, or donate the money directly to organizations such as Toys for Tots.

DOOR-TO-DOOR DELICIOUSNESS

During the first week of December, leave order forms in the mailboxes of nearby friends and neighbors, offering fresh cupcakes delivered to their doorstep on National Cupcake Day, December 15. On the order form, include a list of the flavors, if you and your friends plan on offering a variety. Include your email address and instruct your neighbors and friends to email their orders and their preferred time of delivery. Once all your orders are in, you can coordinate with your friends to determine how many cupcakes need to be baked, how many of each flavor based on the orders you've received, and who will bake what. If you invite twelve friends to help with the fundraiser, have each friend bake a dozen, and you'll be able to fulfill orders for 144 cupcakes!

On the morning of December 15, each of your friends will bake and frost a portion of the custom cupcakes ordered. Package the cupcakes individually in pretty cellophane (see the adorable packaging idea on page 165) before heading out with your friends to deliver the deliciousness to your customers. (This is also a great opportunity to do some old-fashioned door-to-door holiday caroling!) At the end of the day, take the money from your sales and go on a shopping spree to buy toys for a toy drive. You can find donation boxes everywhere this month: in coffee shops, supermarkets, and at school. Maybe you'll buy an Easy-Bake Oven to support the next generation of superstar bakers!

LET THEM EAT CAKE!

When determining what flavor cupcakes to sell, chocolate is an absolute *must*. Follow this recipe for some classic, delicious chocolate cupcakes with buttercream frosting.

CHOCOLATE CUPCAKES
{Makes about 18 cupcakes}

What You Need
- 2 cups plus 2 tablespoons granulated sugar
- 1¾ cups all-purpose flour
- ¾ cup plus 2 tablespoons unsweetened cocoa powder
- 1½ teaspoons baking powder
- 1½ teaspoons baking soda
- 1½ teaspoons salt
- 2 large eggs
- 1 cup milk
- ½ cup vegetable oil
- 1 tablespoon vanilla
- ¾ cup plus 2 tablespoons boiling water

How to Make It
1. Preheat oven to 375°F.

2. In a large bowl, whisk together sugar, flour, cocoa powder, baking powder, baking soda, and salt.

3. In a separate bowl, whisk together eggs, milk, oil, and vanilla. Whisk the egg mixture into the sugar-flour mixture by hand until combined. Whisk in boiling water just until combined. The batter will be very thin and watery.

4. Fill two 12-cup muffin tins with paper liners and spray lightly with cooking spray.

5. Pour the batter into the cups until they are almost full.

6. Bake until a tester inserted into a cupcake comes out clean, 25 to 30 minutes in a conventional oven.

7. Cool in pan 10 minutes; remove to a wire rack to cool completely.

8. Be sure to wait until they are completely cooled before frosting.

BUTTERCREAM FROSTING
{Makes enough for 24 cupcakes}

What You Need
- 4 sticks unsalted butter, softened
- Approximately 3 cups powdered sugar

MAKE A PIPING BAG BY FILLING A PLASTIC SANDWICH BAG WITH FROSTING AND THEN TRIMMING ONE CORNER'S TIP WITH SCISSORS.

Splash of vanilla extract

Food coloring (optional)

Sprinkles or candy (optional)

Dash of salt, to taste

How to Make It

1. Using an electric mixer on low speed, beat butter until it starts to loosen up. Slowly add the powdered sugar, adding more to taste.

2. Add the vanilla extract, and then increase the speed to medium high to beat for around 2 minutes, until it is light in color and fluffy.

3. Add food coloring as desired.

4. Use a piping bag or other decorative icer to add your special flair.

CUPCAKE PACKAGING

Use this simple but lovely packaging to keep your cupcakes from getting squished. Your customers will appreciate the special attention to their orders.

What You Need

Clear plastic 9-ounce cups

Clear cellophane cut to 8-inch squares

Ribbon

Plastic spoons

How to Make It

1. Plop the completed cupcake into the plastic cup. It should be snug.

2. Cut ribbon strips for each individual cupcake order that you have, each around 16 inches long. Lay out the ribbon and center the spoon on top. Tie a single knot to secure the ribbon on the spoon handle.

3. Center the cup with the cupcake inside in the middle of the cellophane square and gather its opposite corners at the top.

4. Gather the cellophane near the rim of the cup.

5. Tie the ribbon in a bow around the gathered cellophane to close it, with the spoon facing out.

35

Bingo Month:
Bingo to Go

BRING YOUR FRIENDS AND A DIY HOLIDAY BINGO GAME TO VISIT A SENIOR CITIZENS' HOME.

I know this might sound obvious, but it's easy to forget that every single elderly person in your life, whether a family member, neighbor, or local shopkeeper, was once your age. And when they were, chances are that some really interesting stuff was happening in the world. Sitting down with someone from a different generation and talking to them about their life can expand our horizons and change the way we see the world. And we might even change their perspective too.

In December, a few members of my a cappella group, the Unaccompanied Minors, sing carols at a veterans' home. My brother and his friends also carol at four or five retirement homes each year. But since singing isn't in everyone's comfort zone, I did a little research and discovered that December happens to be Bingo Month: the perfect opportunity to show the senior members of our community just how much we respect and appreciate them. Bingo is also a lot more interactive than performing songs for people. You get to strike up a conversation, ask some questions, get a little insight, and maybe crack a few jokes. You might want to arm yourself with a few conversation starters first (see below), but with bingo as the icebreaker, you'll be just fine.

LET'S BINGO!

Reach out to a retirement community or even a seniors' nursing home near you to see if you can host a Bingo Social Event for their residents. Or if you don't have anything like this in your town, host an event at your own home and invite your grandparents or elderly friends and neighbors. Donate admission proceeds to a charity for the elderly.

CONVERSATION STARTERS

Here are some pointers on having a good conversation (great for bingo nights and any get-together). Avoid asking questions that demand specific facts or details. Stick to indirect questions that have no right or wrong answers. Ask questions about their past.

Practice using the five Ws: who, what, where, when, and why. Throw in a how or two.

Try out some of my sample questions for seniors:

When you were a kid, what did you do for fun?

What was school like?

What's the best vacation you ever took?

What was your first job?

Who was your hero, growing up?

What world events affected you most?

WHITE ELEPHANT BINGO KIT

Brighten up this bingo game with a holiday twist. Play a round of White Elephant Bingo! Ask each of your guests to bring in a few small gifts from the dollar store and wrap them in festive paper. A range of practical and silly gifts works best. When you get together with the seniors, offer the first bingo winner their choice of gifts and instruct them to open it. The next winner opens their gift and has the option to switch gifts with any previous winner. Every winner, including the first winner, is entitled to one switch. The round ends when the gifts are gone. Before you and your guests head out to visit the seniors, get together for some holiday cheer and assemble this Bingo Kit to take with you.

1. Download bingo cards online and print onto sturdy cardstock or pick up a traditional bingo game at a discount store.

2. Supply decorative scrapbook paper, glittery paper, trims, markers, and glue so that your guests can get creative and make beautiful, one-of-a-kind matting for the bingo cards. You can leave the cards behind as a gift for the seniors to reuse.

3. Colorful ink bingo daubers can be found at a dollar store or get creative: since it's December, use peppermint holiday candies or red and green foil-wrapped chocolate kisses or gumdrops to mark your spaces.

4. Download a free bingo caller app on your smartphone.

5. Wrap the white elephant prizes in festive paper. Some prizes might be hand lotion, tea, silly socks, or a deck of cards. Check out the May Day PhilanthroParty on page 60 for more gift ideas for seniors!

36

National Letter–Writing Day: Write Away Party

HOLD A TEA AND LETTER-WRITING PARTY TO REINFORCE MEANINGFUL CONNECTIONS.

Even though technology is supercool and has revolutionized pretty much every aspect of society, one thing that bums me out about our digital world is the lost art of writing letters. There's something so beautiful and personal about a handwritten letter. Since we're so used to receiving messages in pixel form, reading a letter reminds you that there's an actual person with real feelings behind the words. Also, stationery is the greatest thing ever! My obsession with stationery is a little bit unhealthy. Seriously, I'll walk into a stationery store and lose an entire day.

December 7 is National Letter-Writing Day, which I believe is an important and necessary day to celebrate. So turn back time a few decades, invite your friends over for tea, and host a letter-writing afternoon. Writing a letter to another person is such a thoughtful and honest

expression of kindness, and I believe that doing something good for your best friend or your neighbor is sometimes just as important as doing something good for someone who lives on the other side of the globe. It's all about spreading kindness, which also fosters kindness within yourself.

WRITE ON!

To get you started, I've come up with a list of ideas on how to approach letter writing. It can be a bit daunting for you and your guests to just sit down and write. It has become a lost art form to our generation, and it takes practice, but with these tips, you and your friends will be able to jump right in. I've also got an awesome craft for making your own pressed-flower stationery (see page 171)!

LETTER-WRITING INSTRUCTIONS
Explore the lost art of letter writing, starting with these three addressees.

1. Yourself. That's right; compose a letter to your seven-year-old self, your seventy-seven-year-old self, or yourself in seven years (or any other point in your life).

2. Somebody meaningful who is close to you. This could be a best friend, a family member, a significant other (wink-wink, nudge-nudge), or even your pet! (Letters to humans are encouraged because they are more appreciative of the time and thought.)

3. Somebody meaningful who is *not* close to you. This one is important! Express your feelings for a person you've lost touch with or maybe someone you've never met. Write to a teacher who inspired you. Leave a letter in the mailbox of an elderly neighbor, inviting them to lunch. Send your gratitude to a soldier who has risked their life for your country. (If you choose to do this, consider sending your letter to Operation Gratitude, an organization that assembles care packages for soldiers.)

PRESSED FLOWER STATIONERY

What You Need

Small fresh flowers or pretty leaves

Scissors

Waxed paper

Heavy books

Tweezers

One 8 x 10-inch sheet of clear label
 stickers

Blank notecards

How to Make It

1. Choose small, clean, dry flowers without brown spots. Snip them close to the base of the stem.

2. Place blossoms facedown between two pieces of wax paper and press between pages in a heavy book. Close the book and add more heavy books on top of it. Don't touch for a week to ten days, when you will reveal delicate pressed flowers.

3. Put label stickers with the sticky side up on a dust-free surface. With tweezers, gently lift flowers and transfer them facedown onto the center of the sticker. Make sure enough of the sticker remains clear to hold to the card.

4. Press sticker gently onto blank notecards.

WRITING SUSTENANCE

Every tea party needs proper, bite-sized treats. Little tea sandwiches are a must. My favorite is cream cheese and cucumber. Fresh strawberries, bite-size brownies, and other teatime treats look as good as they taste and are easy to come by. With a little extra effort, these fresh-baked scones will elevate your tea to a truly first-class experience. Try this easy, tasty, crowd-pleasing recipe!

SIMPLE TEA SCONE RECIPE[1]
{Makes 16 scones}

What You Need

- 3 cups all-purpose flour
- ½ cup granulated sugar
- 5 teaspoons baking powder
- ½ teaspoon salt
- ¾ cup cold butter
- 1 large egg, beaten
- 1 cup cold milk
- ½ teaspoon vanilla extract

How to Make It

1. Preheat oven to 400°F.

2. Lightly grease a baking sheet or line with parchment paper.

3. In a large bowl, combine flour, sugar, baking powder, and salt.

4. Cut in butter.

5. Mix egg, milk, and vanilla in a small bowl. Add to flour mixture and stir just until moistened.

6. Drop dough onto a lightly floured surface. Kneed 4 or 5 times by pressing the heel of your hand into the center of the dough, then folding in half. Repeat 3 or 4 times until the dough isn't sticky. Add flour if needed.

7. Roll into two ½-inch-thick rounds and cut each round into 8 wedges.

8. Place wedges on baking sheet. For crisper edges, leave half an inch of space between wedges. Place closer together for soft edges that stick together.

9. Bake for 15 minutes and let cool on the baking sheet. Top scones with butter, jam, honey, clotted cream, or chocolate-hazelnut spread.

Lulu's Letter to Herself in Seven Years

Dear twenty-five-year-old Lulu,

By now, I expect you might want to be called Sofia, which is your first name, after all. Even though you've always gone by your middle name, Lulu, Mom and Dad thought you'd like a more professional-sounding option, especially now, as an intern in Samantha Power's office at the United Nations. But I really hope you stick with Lulu. I'd hate to think of you in a job where you'd have to become someone other than who you have always been. But then again, maybe the older, wiser Lulu can handle it and deserves a new title to reflect all the new and wonderful things you've become.

You look amazing, by the way! Especially your skin and hair. I'm happy to see that seven years as a vegan is giving you a healthy glow. It's going to be tough to decide between continuing your work at the United Nations and opening up that tea shop in Canada with your cousins. I see your online teas are really popular. Congratulations!

Enjoy New York. Don't ever give up that lease on your cute little studio apartment in Brooklyn, and don't forget to visit Uncle Michael next door. Love to see you are still wearing your great-grandfather Len's raggedy blue cardigan. Some things never change!

Love,
Eighteen-year-old *Lulu*

What Are You Waiting For?

There's one question people always ask me when they hear about LemonAID Warriors: How do you have time for all this? With going to school, doing homework, playing with my band, and spending time with my friends and family, I must have a time machine so I can go back each day and fit it all in, right?

Here is what I tell them: it's not easy! But you can figure it out:

- *Set aside a time to organize.* I like to designate Sundays for all my LemonAID work. A designated day and time means it will always get done, and it means I'm not thinking about it at others times during the week, when I need to focus on something else—like my math test.

- *Don't be afraid to ask for help.* My mom is an absolute lifesaver. She helps me keep up with emails and is an expert when it comes to inventing new, creative party ideas and ways to benefit charities. We make a great team. Whether it's collaborating with a family member or a friend, two heads are almost always better than one—and working together is way more fun, too.

- *Don't overcomplicate.* Start small and build from there. There's no need to be fancy. Design your PhilanthroParties to fit into your life by taking something you are already doing and adding a dash of something you want to change.

- *Get inspired, stay inspired.* Whenever I'm having trouble focusing or making decisions, I like to take a moment and think about the good I'm doing. After my first Water Walk (page 90), I had a confidence crisis. I was worried that I wouldn't be able to repeat its success. I was feeling less motivated and less inspired. Around this time, Blood:Water, the organization I work with, flew me out to Tennessee to speak about my Water Walk. While I was on stage, they brought out a man named Michel, who is a Rwandan activist. Through their common need for water, he united two villages that had been at war for years. He got them to agree to build a well together, which was their first step toward peace. The money I'd raised from my Water Walks had helped fund projects like Michel's. He shook my hand and told me that the people in this small village in Rwanda knew about me and my friends and our efforts to help communities like his. It was the first time I really realized that my little PhilanthroParties in Los Angeles were actually making an impact across seas. The sense of pride and happiness I felt when I met Michel got me out of my slump and still drives my work.

Good luck, PhilanthroPartier! You are ready to start your journey as a change-maker. My greatest hope is that once you start PhilanthroPartying, you'll be more empowered to make a positive impact on the world around you for the rest of your life.

Don't forget to write! I would love to hear from you—any triumphs, questions, or concerns. Come find me at LemonAIDWarriors.com.

I can't wait to see what you do!

Lulu Cerone
xo

ACKNOWLEDGMENTS

I started writing this book when I was fifteen years old, but the story began five years earlier, with my fifth-grade class and our teacher, Mrs. Yeager, at the Wesley School in North Hollywood, California. Wesley students were the original LemonAID Warriors who helped create the first PhilanthroParties, and I am so grateful for the time we spent together. Thank you to my dear friends at the Archer School for Girls, especially to my class of 2017 sisters Stella Gage, Elizabeth Zinman, and Gabby Weltman, my go-to volunteers. And thanks to the talented Carly Feldman for providing the recipes for this book.

Thank you to the first people who mentored a quiet twelve-year-old girl and gave her the courage and skill to take her ideas seriously: Denise Restauri, Addie Daddio, Mariama Camara, Mike Lenda, Jena Lee Nardella, Dan Haseltine, Jillian Howard Bowman, Nile Rodgers, Nancy Hunt, and everyone at the We Are Family Foundation. Thank you to Paul DiMeo for building me the ultimate LemonAID Stand, and to Larry Lerner, Ken Wilton, and Allyson Maida for taking care of business.

It takes a brave and patient person to deal with a teenage, first-time author. I am so grateful to Clelia Gore for her wisdom and guidance and for connecting me to a talented support team, including Lucy Keating and my editor, Lindsay Easterbrooks-Brown.

I'm especially grateful to Renee Bowen for her beautiful photographs, to Jill and Emma Nelson for their art direction and crafting genius, and to Elisa Rothstein for the food styling. And thank you to all of my Little Star friends for a lifetime of love and support.

My family is everything to me. My brother Jasper's generous heart knows no limits. Thank you, Jasper, for doing the hard behind-the-scenes work and for recruiting your amazing friends. Most of all, thank you to Mom and Dad for showing me how to take what's in my heart and in my head and make it real.

PHILANTHROPARTY PLANNING GUIDE

Still haven't decided on your cause? See my tips in the Introduction. If you already know who you want to help, use this section to help get organized for your party.

CHOOSING A CHARITY

Once you have identified a cause that you feel passionate about supporting, it usually makes sense to find an organization that's already working on the issue. Typically, charitable organizations are happy to receive—and give—support: they can tell you where and how to make donations, offer volunteer opportunities, and provide speakers and other contacts.

To make your list, start with the internet. A Google search on your chosen cause will probably reveal a long list of organizations. For example, most of the kids who come to me for mentorship want to help animals as their first cause. When we Google "Animal Rescue," dozens of small local animal shelters and rescue organizations pop up, along with hundreds of huge national animal advocacy and rescue organizations. So the next step is to decide if you want to go big or small.

The benefit of a large organization is name recognition. If you are raising money, it's often more comfortable for people to donate to organizations that they recognize. The larger organizations also have terrific resources on their websites, including information to help educate yourself and your volunteers on the need that you are trying to address. Large organizations usually already have events and activities that you can join in on all year long. I have partnered with large organizations many times and have really benefited from their vast resources, such as tool kits for fundraising and downloadable materials to help publicize and market events. Many organizations even have online fundraising platforms already set up so that I can easily create my own fundraising page.

Things run very smoothly with larger organizations because they have a solid infrastructure in place to make things easier.

Still, sometimes, smaller is better! When I partner with local organizations, their websites may not have slick videos and downloadable action plans to help me organize my events, but what they lack in infrastructure they make up for in the personnel department. Partnering with local organizations usually means you get to work directly with the founder. You can form a really special mentorship relationship and get a lot of personal support. When I partner with smaller organizations, they often send representatives to my events or to my classroom to talk about the cause and share personal stories, which makes a deeper impact on my PhilanthroParty guests.

Whatever route you take, it is important to research the organization you choose to support. Charities are supposed to follow certain rules to make sure they spend the donation money on the cause they are promising to help. Charities can be effective or not, depending on many different factors: leadership, funding, organization, and honesty, to name a few. If your main goal is to really help people in need, then don't skip this essential step: make sure you partner with a reputable organization by researching, or vetting, its business practices. Check CharityNavigator.com to see if your charity of interest is in good standing with the law. If it isn't listed, follow the site's instructions on how to vet unlisted charities.

HOW DO I TALK TO A CHARITY?

Once you have chosen your cause and your charitable organization, then it's time to reach out to them. This part can be intimidating. I have to confess, I am oddly terrified of talking on the phone. It comes from years of texting as my main communication mode. Fortunately, email is often the most effective way to make an initial introduction.

When emailing the organization, remember to make it formal, friendly, and short:

1. Introduce yourself.

2. Tell them your age.

3. Briefly state why this cause matters to you (including a short personal story, if you have one) and why you chose their organization.

4. Share your PhilanthroParty idea and ask if they have any materials you can share to educate your guests about their work. If you are interested in taking it a step further, you can invite them to your event or ask if they have volunteer opportunities for your age group. (If your first letter feels long, wait until they've responded and invite them to your event or ask about volunteer opportunities in the next note.) Remember, if it's important to you to have a representative at your event in person, reach out before you commit to a date.

When I have taken the time to make personal connections with the people at charities I support, some pretty cool things have happened. One summer we did a music concert PhilanthroParty for a dog rescue organization and invited the founder, Addie Daddio. Next, she invited me to be a guest on her radio show called *Love That Dog Hollywood!* Soon after that, she offered to teach me how to host a radio show, and she eventually produced my own radio show where I got to feature youth activists and young musicians. Making a strong personal connection with a small local charity helped me find an amazing mentor, led me on a valuable journey, and even brought my family a dog!

LET SAFETY (AND COMMON SENSE) BE YOUR GUIDE

Feeling inspired can fill you with energy and do-it-now enthusiasm, which can go a long way to making your PhilanthroParty a success. But remember that your events must also be safe and scheduled at a time that will work for your intended participants. And listen to your common sense: don't ignore that little voice in your head whispering that something may not be safe or may not be allowed! Give yourself enough time to check with someone about what's nagging you.

Given the endless possibilities, some of these considerations may actually help you decide what kind of PhilanthroParties make sense for you.

GET PERMISSION

This may seem like a no-brainer, but *before* you spend any time, energy, or other resources on your party, make sure you have permission to use your venue on the exact date and time you want it. You don't want to risk wasting your time or losing momentum for your cause by having to inform people of a change of venue or date. Even at home, make sure you ask well in advance. Parks, community buildings, and spaces at school may be available for free, but they typically require at least reservations or permits. The rule with using public space: never assume that the space is available; always check!

COOKING

The obvious first: As mentioned earlier in this book, if you aren't already accustomed to using a stove, oven, or sharp kitchen tools, make sure an adult is present. And—while I hope the parties themselves are fun and that the cooking is fun—making food requires care. Whether preparing food for your guests or food to be donated, remember to treat people's food with respect and follow safe and sanitary food preparation practices:

1. Wash your hands before handling any food.

2. Maintain a clean kitchen workspace, wiping down surfaces with bacteria-killing bleach water (1 tablespoon per gallon).

3. Wash fruits and vegetables before using them.

4. Keep ready-to-eat foods away from raw meat and the surfaces you prepare them on.

5. Do not participate if you are sick.

6. If you are working a booth where people are paying for food, make sure you are well stocked with disposable gloves and that duties are assigned so helpers don't handle food after touching money.

Other important safety considerations depend on what you are serving and where. For example, if you're serving lemonade or another cold drink, a scoop for ice should be kept in a container outside the ice bucket, so the handle can't contaminate ice that's going into people's drinks. Foods containing meat and dairy need to be refrigerated or put on ice if they are left out for more than a couple hours—especially in hot places. The list goes on. Check out the United States Department of Agriculture's website. They have a great Food Safety Education page that will answer all of your questions. While you're selling food or serving it, it's also a good idea to keep a list of food ingredients handy in case someone with a food restriction asks for it. If you aren't sure whether something has peanuts or dairy or gluten, it's always better to be safe than sorry. Take it from me—I have a long list of food allergies and restrictions, and I'm constantly asking about ingredients.

LULU'S PHILANTHROPARTY CHECKLIST

Once you've decided on a party theme and cause, here's a weekly checklist to make sure you're fully prepared. While many of the PhilanthroParties in this book can be easily put together on short notice, some are more involved and require planning. Spread out the tasks over a number of weeks, so you are not overwhelmed as the party date approaches.

SEVEN WEEKS OUT: FINALIZE DATE

Before you do anything, you need to secure a date. You can start by cross-referencing your family calendar and school calendar. Once you find an open date, it's not a bad idea to check to see that it isn't conflicting with any of your guests' birthdays. If you are hosting in a location outside your home, secure your venue for your chosen date. Next, you need to clear that date with your support team. Who are you counting on to help you make this a success? Make sure that date is clear for your volunteers and adult supervisors. If you are inviting a guest speaker, send an invitation to them as soon as you finalize the date.

SIX WEEKS OUT: RECRUIT COHOSTS (IF YOU WANT THEM) AND A SUPPORT TEAM

Do you work better alone? Or do you prefer to work in a group? Either way, you are going to need some help. Decide how much of the work you'd like to delegate and start recruiting helpers. Pick friends with different strengths to increase the fun and assign them tasks based on their talents. Hold a planning meeting and brainstorm ideas.

- The Organizers: These people deal with the planning and details.

- The Foodies: A perfect job for food lovers everywhere. They plan the menu and serve the food.

- The Photographers: You'll want to remember the day, so make sure somebody is capturing the action! You may also want to use the photos to continue to promote your cause after the party. Before you share or post any photograph, make sure you get permission from everyone who appears in the photo.

- The Cheerleaders: They are the life of the party! Cheerleaders spread the word about the cause. If you are not a confident public speaker, then this other person is particularly important. This is a person who might enjoy learning details about the cause and giving a little speech or answering questions about the cause at your party. This person might also want to make announcements at school or create marketing strategies and do local outreach to get local businesses involved.

Optimize the experience for your volunteers! Many schools require a set amount of community service hours. Contact your school and get permission to grant your volunteers community service hours for planning, setting up, and cleaning up.

FIVE WEEKS OUT: DETERMINE SUPPLIES AND BUDGET

Think about the food, activities, and decorations you want at your party and then write a list of the ingredients and supplies needed to make your vision a reality. Mark off the items you already have and make a separate list of the things you need. Spend the next two weeks finding the best deals to keep your costs low. Check dollar stores and thrift shops. Ask friends and neighbors if you can borrow things you might not have but don't want to buy. Add up the cost of the things you will need to buy to fulfill this list, making sure items are within your budget. If you have gone over your budget, start making cuts or substitutions. Sometimes, you may need to order items online. It may take a while for the item to ship to you, so get your order in early.

FOUR WEEKS OUT: SEND INVITATIONS

This is a good week to create and send invitations. You'll likely get a bigger turnout if you invite your guests four weeks ahead of time. But that's not always possible, so don't worry if you can't get it together this far in advance.

Include information about your cause along with the details of your PhilanthroParty. If you are collecting cash donations, I strongly recommend using an online invitation site like ECHOage.com, because guests can make charitable donations online as part of the actual invitation when they RSVP. Punchbowl.com invitations also include an option to contribute cash online. This way, even if guests can't make it to your party, they still have the option to contribute. Plus, it takes away the hassle of dealing with actual cash on the day of your party. If you prefer paper invitations, you can still set up an online donation campaign using platforms like CrowdRise.com or Fundly.com. Be aware that these sites often charge a small percentage fee.

Write a Press Release

Raising awareness for your cause can be just as important as raising funds. I know I keep saying this, but it's true. So go ahead and tell the media about your event and ask them to help spread the word about your cause and about PhilanthroPartying. Big or small, your PhilanthroParty is a story worth sharing. Write a simple press release and send it to local newspapers, magazines, and television news stations. Magazines need to get the information at least four weeks in advance. Television news stations often have a tip line on their websites where you can submit your press release. Or you can find out who produces the morning news or evening news and send your press release to the producer.

Here is a simple press release template to follow: The first paragraph simply states the five *W*s:

Who: Give your name, age, and contact information.

What and Why: Explain your PhilanthroParty and the cause you are supporting.

When: Give the date and time of the event.

Where: Give the address of the event.

I live in Los Angeles, where thousands of people compete to get on the news every day, but my simple press release emails have been very successful. My events have landed on the morning and evening news three times. If your town is smaller than LA, then you have a really good chance of getting your story out

there and raising awareness for your cause. Make sure to tell your guests to get permission from their parents to be on the news, just in case.

THREE WEEKS OUT: SHOP AND PREP

Finish buying all the items on that list of ingredients and supplies you made when you planned your budget. Hold off on buying any fresh ingredients needed for your recipes until a few days before your party. Once you have all of your materials, look for things you can make ahead of time, like decorations, goody bags, posters, and signs. If your party includes a crafting activity, you can prepare and organize the materials that your guests will need.

TWO WEEKS OUT: SEND INVITATION REMINDERS AND CONDUCT RECIPE TESTS

If you sent out an invitation four weeks in advance, this is a good time to send out a reminder to those who have not yet confirmed their attendance. If you used an online invitation platform, managing your guest list is easy. An accurate headcount is crucial when finalizing plans for food and activities. This is also a good week to test new recipes if you are serving something you have never made before.

ONE WEEK OUT: ADD FINAL TOUCHES

You've done all the hard prep work! Now it's time to put it all together. Pretend you are a guest entering your party and do a walk-through. This will help you determine the best place to set things up. You will be surprised at how many decisions you will need to make ahead of time and how many issues you will need to solve before your big day. Here are some important questions you should ask yourself while "walking through" your party:

Should there be balloons or signs visible from the street, so guests know where the party is taking place?

Should I have a donation table or display with brochures and information about the cause? Where should this table go for ultimate impact?

Where can I set out the food so that it is protected from direct sunlight and bugs? For perishables, how am I going to keep them hot or cold and safe to consume?

Where will the craft table go? Do I need to find a shady spot?

What is my backup plan in case it rains?

This is also a good time to reconfirm with your volunteers, speakers, and venue.

Visual Aids

It's a good idea to make posters with facts about your cause and hang them around your party space. That way you can educate your guests on your cause even if you don't have a speaker and don't want to give a speech. Sometimes the charities you are supporting can send you posters and visual aids if you ask them in advance. They also might be able to send you brochures that you can display or include in goody bags. Think about planning a short presentation using videos or a PowerPoint to help your guests understand why the cause is so important.

THE DAY OF YOUR PARTY

You've made it! If you've been following these steps, setup will be super easy because all of your decisions have been made and everything has been prepared ahead of time. Food preparation will be the most complicated part of your setup today. Fresh food should be handled the day of your party, but you can probably make most of your dishes the day before.

POST-PHILANTHROPARTY: AMPLIFY YOUR IMPACT

Once the fun is over, calculate your social impact and spread the word! This way, you can raise even more awareness about your cause. Plus, if people hear about the success of your PhilanthroParty, they might be inspired to host their own. Post about your party on social media. Put together a video and share it with your community. Write an article for your school's paper. Ask the charity you supported if they would like you to guest-blog on their website or if they would like to use any of your photos as content for their social media outlets. News sources love to feature awesome work being done in their communities. Sharing your experience is the best tool for encouraging others to party with a purpose. (I'd love to hear about your PhilanthroParty. Email your pictures or videos to me at lemonaidwarriors@gmail.com, so I can feature your work on my website.)

Thank-You Cards

As you've probably noticed, I'm a huge fan of online invitations because they make it so easy to manage your guest list and collect donations. Plus, with a few clicks, you can send thank-you notes to all of your guests.

When drafting your thank-you cards, consider including facts and figures that measure the social impact of your PhilanthroParty. Add up dollars raised, items donated, volunteer hours completed, petition signatures collected, and anything else that applies to your party. Your guests will truly understand the importance of their efforts when they can measure their impact. If you had friends volunteer to help you with party preparations or during the party, it's always nice to send additional handwritten thank-you notes to them. Don't forget adults who may have done some extra driving, run errands, supervised activities, or helped clean up, which is everyone's least favorite part!

SLACKTIVISM ISN'T SO BAD

Have you heard of slacktivism? To be described as a slacktivist is to be negatively criticized as being someone who substitutes internet advocacy for traditional volunteerism and philanthropy. A slacktivist is sometimes seen as lazy for pointing and clicking to support social and political change instead of putting in the physical labor of hands-on volunteering and fundraising. But you know what? I wouldn't consider myself a lazy person, and I'm actually proud to call myself a slacktivist!

Sometimes, I admit, the thought of pulling off a service project or event is overwhelming. And most of the time, I'm just too *busy*. Even the smallest event is sometimes nearly impossible because of school and homework and afterschool activities. It's upsetting when you really do *want* to help, but your schedule gets in the way. A huge reason we don't take action is lack of time. So why not hurdle that obstacle by embracing the idea that you can create real change as you scroll through your phone while lounging in your pajamas or sitting on the bus or waiting in line at the coffee shop. Just because it's that easy doesn't mean it's not effective. Slacktivism to the rescue!

In our lifetime, technology is going to be our most powerful tool to create social and political change. We've already seen the magical powers of social media raise over a hundred million dollars for ALS with the Ice Bucket Challenge;[1] mobilize rescue efforts after natural disasters like the 2010 earthquake in Haiti; highlight issues like the racial divide in Ferguson, Missouri; and overthrow governments during the Arab Spring uprisings in Tunisia, Egypt, Libya, and Syria. Technology lets you amplify your voice and be heard by your friends, community—potentially millions of people. It allows you to put pressure on those in charge and create huge shifts in our world.

If you are ever looking for a cause that really inspires you, slacktivism can be your gateway. It gives you a greater awareness about local and global needs, which might connect you to a cause that fires you up and leads you to take further action. Everyone has to start somewhere. Here are my easy steps to help you harness the power of technology to do good:

1. Follow news platforms, organizations, and interesting people who are doing cool things. Follow them on Twitter and Instagram, like their Facebook pages, and download their apps to make sure important and interesting information is a part of your feed, along with all the other things you subscribe to. You never know! One of those stories might hit you on an emotional level and inspire you to take action. Scrolling through Twitter or checking Facebook doesn't have to be mindless entertainment. It just might be the thing that sets you on your path as an activist.

2. Share news stories that interest or infuriate you: information on causes you care about, links to local community service events, and anything else that sparks your compassion. Raising awareness is immeasurably valuable. Starting a conversation in your community of friends might spark ideas. You may not be able to act directly to help out the causes

you read about, but by sharing, someone else might just be able to take it to the next level. Expose the work, stories, causes, and efforts of people you admire. Don't underestimate the power of sharing. Chances are, if you read a news story and it makes you want to cry or scream or break something, it will probably make someone else feel the same way. That's how movements are started! Sharing helps causes gain strength in numbers and inch their way toward change.

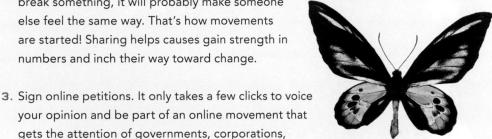

3. Sign online petitions. It only takes a few clicks to voice your opinion and be part of an online movement that gets the attention of governments, corporations, and global leaders who are in a position to make real change. You can join platforms like Change.org or Causes.com and get emails about trending petitions so you stay updated. Or start your own online campaign or petition. Sign, share, and be part of a movement that gets the attention of people who can truly create change.

4. Write your city council, your senator, the head of a major corporation, the president, or anyone else who is in a position to fix something you want fixed. You might be thinking you have no idea who your senator or assembly person is or how to contact them. And most of us don't have a clue about which bills we can support to help make change on a legislative level. It may seem overwhelming, but here's the good news: there's an organization that I love that sets it all up for you! They mostly deal with global poverty issues, but that's a great place for you to start. They're called One.org. Subscribe! They will send you texts and alerts about issues coming up. Type in your zip code, and they automatically send you your representative's information. With one text, they will even connect you directly to the White House, so you can make a call. That's it—easy! After you get in the habit of voicing your opinion to leaders through One.org, you will see how easy it is and will likely start doing it on your own.

Every little bit helps.

A WORD FROM LULU'S MOM TO PARENTS AND EDUCATORS

Partying for a cause. Sounds like a fun idea that most parents and educators can get behind, but what if the cause isn't fun? The stolen girls of Nigeria. Terminal illness. Natural disasters. Exposing our children to tragedy contradicts the parental instinct to create a protective bubble around them because, after all, kids are not meant to shoulder the burden of the world's ills.

This is a challenge all parents and educators face. Do we shield our kids from the human-rights horrors in the media? Is there an appropriate age and method to expose them to the issues affecting their world? Can children actually be helpful when a situation seems hopeless, or are their gestures purely symbolic?

If fundraising is fun, does it trivialize other people's pain?

As a parent, I wrestle with these questions, and so do my kids' teachers. Service was never a big part of my childhood, so I didn't have a blueprint for my children, outside the fierce protective instincts of a mom. But no matter how hard I tried to make Lulu feel safe, my daughter and her friends—at a very young age—had an acute awareness and curiosity about the things they saw in their daily lives that seemed unfair or needed fixing. They had powerful emotional reactions that were impossible to ignore.

The trash on the beach made them angry. The homeless people at the park across from their school made them really sad. The dogs they saw in our overflowing shelters broke their hearts. And as much as I tried to shield Lulu from negative images in the media, I couldn't always be there to control her environment. As her access to technology increased, so did her exposure to the even harsher realities of the world outside our community. So I decided that if I couldn't shield my young daughter from the world, I could at least help her make sense of the information she was receiving.

I started conversations to allow her to express her questions and feelings. I answered her questions as honestly as I could. But I noticed that, despite these discussions, she still felt unsettled. Part of it was the fear that something bad like that might also happen to her. Even adults can feel helpless when faced with issues plaguing our society, but when you are nine years old, it's safe to say that feeling is multiplied. But even more concerning to me was the fact that Lulu felt powerless in the face of those overwhelming realities.

When I saw fear creep into these discussions, I started to ask her, "What can you and your friends do about it *right now*?" I was amazed at how fast they came up with answers. "We can have a lemonade stand." "We can collect warm blankets." "We can write letters to the president." The actual impact of these small gestures didn't move the needle toward solving the issues, but they changed my daughter in a seismic way. They empowered her to take control of an out-of-control world and help others along the way. Taking action, for my daughter, is now a second-nature impulse when her compassion is sparked.

I know many people feel that a child's small efforts are only symbolic—they'll never fix the problem or change the world—but kindness is never symbolic. It touches everyone around you. This book about PhilanthroParties grew out of Lulu's impulse to join together with friends and take action to fix problems. Partying would not have been my adult response to address sensitive, serious issues, but the idea took hold in our community. Parents accepted these PhilanthroParties as kid-friendly versions of the charity galas, and fundraising dinners that adults are already familiar with. PhilanthroParties are not meant to celebrate in the face of tragedy. They are meant to celebrate a young person's power to spread kindness and create positive change.

My hardest job, as a parent, is to stay out of the way. When Lulu and her friends are left to pick the cause and invent creative ways to contribute, their ideas resonate stronger with their peer group than if a grownup chooses the activities. Taking ownership of the event boosts their pride, confidence, and self-esteem. I've found that parents are most helpful as facilitators. We can facilitate the conversation about the issues and frame them in a way that is appropriate for the child's emotional maturity level. And we can facilitate a safe environment, a manageable budget, and the organizational details that are beyond a young person's skill set.

Surprisingly, the easiest job in facilitating these PhilanthroParties is fitting them into our calendar. When I used to try to organize a community service project for our family, it was nearly impossible to squeeze it in between sports tournaments, music lessons, family obligations, and school demands. I often just gave up. Now, Lulu looks at what we already have planned on our calendar, puts her special PhilanthroParty twist on it, and turns any gathering into a chance to give back.

For educators, scheduling isn't that easy. As a community service teacher's aid, I have enormous sympathy for teachers who have a full load of curriculum obligations and precious little free time to add a service project. But integrating PhilanthroParties into their existing curriculum has been working out really well for teachers across the country. Classes in literature, history, science, and social studies bring up many issues of social injustice or environmental concerns for students. Incorporating a PhilanthroParty as a group project at the end of a unit can be very effective.

Ms. Marshall, a sixth-grade teacher in Darien, Connecticut, saw Lulu on the Nickelodeon Halo Awards and asked her to help them come up with PhilanthroParty ideas at the end of a difficult social justice unit. Small groups of students each chose an issue that resonated strongly with them. In lieu of a traditional group presentation, each group led the whole class to come together to take action. There was a letter-writing PhilanthroParty to thank their governor for ending veteran homelessness in Connecticut. There was a craft PhilanthroParty when they made animal-cruelty-free beauty products. And, to Ms. Marshall's surprise, the projects spread around the whole school. For example, when a clothing drive PhilanthroParty was planned, kids from other grades heard about it and brought in bags of clothing to contribute. When the students made friendship bracelets for their anti-bullying PhilanthroParty, other kids asked about them on the schoolyard, which gave the sixth graders a chance to talk about their cause and spread the word. Ms. Marshall shared with me,

> The students really experienced firsthand that they were the spark that started it all! They learned that by taking action and putting that energy out there, other people (kids and adults) would get involved in a big way. On the day of each PhilanthroParty, the students came in eager, excited, and prepared. And after a great PhilanthroParty, students from other groups congratulated them with sincerity and respect.

Lulu's PhilanthroParty book is simply an extension of her desire to share a vibrant, meaningful part of her childhood that has enriched the lives of anyone who has ever attended or hosted a PhilanthroParty. It has been my honor to work beside her friends who formed an army of young LemonAID Warriors and started this movement in our community. They inspire me every day. If there are any questions left about the merits of a PhilanthroParty, the simplest response is this: No act of kindness is ever wasted. Any action a child takes to address another's need is a worthy action. No matter how small.

Lisa Cerone

Parent Advisor of Educators Consortium for Service Learning,
Community Service Committee Chair at the Wesley School, the Archer School for Girls, the
Buckley School